My Spirit Is Not Religious™

My Spirit Is Not Religious™

A Guide To Living Your Authentic Life

Tina Sacchi

NEW YORK

My Spirit Is Not Religious™
A Guide To Living *Your* Authentic Life

ISBN 978-1-61448-368-7 paperback
ISBN 978-1-61448-369-4 eBook
Library of Congress Control Number: 2012947876

Morgan James Publishing
The Entrepreneurial Publisher
5 Penn Plaza, 23rd Floor
New York City, New York 10001
(212) 655-5470 office • (516) 908-4496 fax
www.MorganJamesPublishing.com

Cover Design by:
Brenda Haun
BHaundesigns@gmail.com

Interior Design by:
Bonnie Bushman
bonnie@caboodlegraphics.com

In an effort to support local communities, raise awareness and funds, Morgan James Publishing donates a percentage of all book sales for the life of each book to Habitat for Humanity Peninsula and Greater Williamsburg.

Get involved today, visit
www.MorganJamesBuilds.com.

To God, with all my love.

Living YOUR Authentic Life
By Tina Sacchi

A powerful force called the Great Spirit,
In our heart it dwells.
Its unconditional loving nudges,
Will ensure that everyone excels.

You may know it, see it or feel it,
The strength is immensely powerful and the love is pure.
To authentically live YOUR life,
Is your birthright, now and forevermore.

Being a peaceful, loving teacher to everyone,
Is essential in spiritual growth.
To commune and celebrate with like-minded people,
Is our spiritual oath.

Knowing that WE ARE ALL ONE,
Regardless of all the beliefs in this world that exist.
Living YOUR spiritual life in peace and in love,
Is a desire that will forever persist.

Table of Contents

PART I. A Different Way to Feel God

Part I explores the history of religious beliefs and stories and the ways they continue to be passed down through the generations, regardless of whether or not they make sense or have practical application for modern believers. Discussions include the issues, challenges, and negative impacts such hand-me-down beliefs we have in today's world.

Part II. To Come Out or Stay Inside the Spiritual Closet

Part II Introduces the meaning of "spiritual closet" and explores the process of spiritual self-discovery. Readers are introduced to the concept of coming out of their closets and provided with guidelines and exercises to facilitate such a transformation.

Part III. Tools for Moving Forward on Your Spiritual Journey and Eliminating Religious Guilt

Part III offers practical guidance to help readers deal with the virtually inevitable guilt that accompanies leaving one's ancestral, familial, or cultural religious traditions. Readers will be comforted that they are not alone and will receive practical tools they can implement to better adjust to their newly adopted spiritual paths.

Part IV. Staying on Spiritual Task....
Spiritual Maintenance for a Spiritual Lifestyle

Part IV deals with the challenges of growing and flourishing in one's newly chosen spiritual life. Discussions include advice for reaching out to spiritual guides, being patient with oneself, acknowledging the impermanence of this life, and living one's purpose.

To find out more about **Tina Sacchi**, her availability as a speaker, retreat facilitator, products, services, healthy tips, recipes, free podcasts from her international radio shows, please visit:

www.**TinaSacchi**.com

***Bonus: Download free exercises,
meditations, tips, etc. from
www.TinaSacchi.com***

Which Church Is the Right Church?

**The truth is simple.
If it were complicated, everyone would understand it.**
— Author unknown

You may have come to this book one of several ways ...

- Perhaps you have many questions and are reading it behind someone's back, in fear of getting caught – at which time you'll need to deal with judgment day.
- Perhaps you've done the religion thing, but religion is not working for you because you know there is more.
- Perhaps you've had no religious upbringing, but your spirit is now searching, and you are soul-searching.

My dear ones, you are beginning to step onto your spiritual path simply by reading this book. Regardless of what brought you here, I welcome you with spiritual arms. The purpose of this book is to enable you to eliminate religious guilt, while enlightening you and guiding you toward the spirituality that works for you. To help you live as a free and loving spirit. To give you permission to feel and believe there are easier roads to spirituality than religion.

There truly is a spiritual way, a way with God, not apart from God. If there is no one in your life you can talk with about this important subject, this book provides exercises and the Points of Reflection that will help you reach your spiritual path on your terms. You are now free to create peace and love within your true belief system.

If you have a friend or two with whom you can share this conversation and information, perhaps together you can use this book as a study guide, meeting periodically to read and discuss the chapters/sections and do the exercises. In coming together, you will be able to share, support, cheer, encourage, and love one another along your shared spiritually enlightening journeys.

Much of the material in this book comes from my own as well as my clients' and students' experiences with religion and spirituality. The point of referencing these stories is to illuminate the fact that you are not alone. So many of us have lived this that it is nearly universal.

The purpose of this book is for you to see for yourself and show others that life really is simple. It's not about fear, or power – it's all about love. I truly believe that we come to Earth to learn to love ourselves unconditionally, and in turn, we are able to love others unconditionally, too. Although easy to say and write, this is the most difficult thing we will ever do in our lives. Think about loving everything about yourself unconditionally … whether physically, emotionally, mentally, or spiritually. Think about loving and embracing all your strengths and weaknesses. If it seems easy, that's great –

but chances are, if you're like most people, it's not so easy to embrace and love your total self. This seems to be a universal characteristic of the human experience.

Spirituality gives us unity. It provides us the truth that we are God, because God lives in us. God is in us, not somewhere else outside of us, above or around us. God is not judging us when we do something wrong. How do we even define the meaning of wrong, anyway?

A loving God receives no satisfaction in taking revenge against us for our mistakes and the lessons we've come here to learn. I believe we are spiritual beings, enrolled in study at this Earth school. We have incarnated onto this plane to learn, grow, and love. To learn to love ourselves unconditionally and love others in the same way. Upon death, we leave this body, and this physical experience ends. However our spirit lives on. Our spirit never dies.

The fact is that we need the dark so we can see the light. We need the bad so we can know what is good. We need those difficult times and relationships in order to appreciate good times and loving relationships.

Spirituality presents us with some challenging questions: What is the purpose of life? And, more importantly, what is the purpose of *my* life?

Most organized religion has separated us from our spirit, from God. Religion uses a weapon called fear to gain power and control over people. Fear is not life-giving; quite the contrary. Fear constricts us. If you think about it, the cause of most war boils down to religious issues which arise out of a desire to control that is bred from fear, fear of something or someone different. Plain and simple, we're killing each other over these ridiculous religious beliefs. We're killing each other in God's name. Religion has God all wrong. There are easier paths to spirituality than religion.

So if we are God, and God resides within all of us, we can access him at all times. Our spiritual bible is constantly within reach because we *are* the spiritual bible. No, not the Bible that was written, edited, and rewritten by man, decades after the events it claims to have recorded. Tell me whether you can write in detail about a year in your life that occurred 20, 50, or 75 years ago? This would be impossible for most of us. Yet many people live according to this Bible – and kill each other over its words. That is not living with God; that is living apart from God.

Would Jesus or any enlightened master such as Buddha or Krishna or even Mother Theresa kill to spread the word of God? Of course not. So why do we?

The spiritual bible consists only of love. Our goal is to live as authentic beings, neither inferior nor superior to one another. We are one; we are divine.

When you look into someone's eyes, you are looking at God. When you finally start to understand this, when you see that you are God and realize that God is omnipresent, living everywhere at the same time, your life will begin to make sense and have more meaning. You will begin to understand that God has many aspects which are depicted through our individuality and uniqueness.

Individuality makes our lives significant and passionate. And through it, we learn from each other. If fear is restricting us, we must merely eliminate it to find out who we really are. We achieve freedom when we face fear, head-on. But religion doesn't want us to find out who we really are because then we'd be directly united with God without an intermediary. Such a discovery would leave religion powerless.

After working with many clients and students, I realized that religion gets them started on a path that is nothing more than a belief. In their spiritual exploration, they begin to realize there must be more than religion, so they step off that path and onto the path of spirituality. They start resonating with the truth of God, that we are all one.

What Would God Do?

Make no mistake. There is nothing wrong with religion if it's practiced with love and kindness. If people follow it and use it with a sense of unity for all humans, it can be great. What saddens me are the millions of people who attend church each week and, upon leaving the services, immediately begin judging themselves and others. They curse the slow cashier at the store, cut off someone in traffic, or complain and gossip about their neighbors or friends. Is this what God would do? Is this what Jesus would do? Act and live as a hypocrite? Is this what they would have us do?

And yet I see this behavior again and again – people who proclaim that Jesus saves, then backstab their fellow human beings. Is this what religion teaches them, that it is appropriate or a good thing to behave this way? I doubt it. So why do so many religious people live this way? Could it be that organized religion is not giving them all the tools they really need in life?

Will the Right Church Please Present Itself?

My husband and I spent years seeking the right church. We attended many of them, in various faiths. But we found each one after the next to be incredibly regimented with rules and fear-based teachings. However, we truly did not feel that all these rules and regulations came from God. We would leave each church/religion even more disillusioned than the one before it. After all our searching, we were sad that we could not find a church to fit our needs.

So I started to meditate more often, inquiring within. I connected with my Higher Self and realized that we are all one.

This was not easy to do after decades of Christian upbringing, schools, sermons, sacraments, and the rest. After all those Sundays of attending service, I no longer chose to do so. But in spite of knowing this change was in service to myself and my spirit, a hand-me-down generational pattern was still making me feel guilty. I knew with all my heart and soul that I was doing the right thing, yet the guilt weighed heavily on me.

My Italian, Roman Catholic parents lived only minutes away, so we belonged to the same church – and, of course, they no longer saw me there. "Why?" was the big question, and I was ill-prepared to answer it. I still was not ready to fully stand in my power, even as I knew I would never go down the path of religion again.

Fortunately, I was busy working and raising kids. My parents knew how hard I worked, how difficult my colicky son was – so they didn't push the issue much, and I hid behind the excuse.

"When is he going to be baptized?" they would chime in periodically.

"Soon," I would say.

My husband and I did ultimately decide to go through with the baptism. It was a celebration of life, and celebrating our son's life was really important to us. Besides, who wanted to hear about the possibility of "limbo" (babies trapped between heaven and hell) if he should – God forbid – happen to die before this ritual took place? It was just easier all the way around to have him baptized and make everyone else happy.

So we did, and we had a joyous, wonderful party to celebrate. And part of me was relieved that my baby's soul was legitimized before my church and community since I wasn't totally certain in my stance with God at that time. Was I religious, spiritual or both? I was still exploring.

The Church of Home

Then came the time to prepare my older son for his first communion. Before being allowed to receive this sacrament, my son had to attend weekly classes and services with at least one parent for a year. So my husband diligently did his duty. Each time they would come home from class, though, my husband would say, "I'm going through this, but I feel so hypocritical. I do not attend church. Why are we doing this, Tina?"

The only answer was guilt, plain and simple. The religious guilt that had been passed on for generations. We were literally going through the motions without engaging our hearts and souls. We were doing it because it was easier to go with everyone else's flow than to create our own. Theirs seemed more powerful than ours. Our parents on both sides were hounding us. Our siblings on both sides were going with that flow. Relatives, friends, and neighbors were all in agreement. We really felt it was us against them. And, quite honestly, we were not yet ready to step into our power.

In the meantime, we continued to search for the right church, the church that would address all our needs. We required our religion and the church members themselves to be open, unconditionally loving, nonjudgmental, flexible in their thought process, and, of course, spiritual. One day, after years of religious education and more years of searching, we came to the conclusion that the church we sought was in our home. My home was my religion. And so that day, I completely surrendered any guilt, excuses, or justifications, and my husband and I decided to dedicate our home as the foundation of our spiritually.

I later realized that my clients and students served as my "church," as well. They came to me for guidance and support, so I created spiritual circles where liked-minded people could come together and grow spiritually. This is how I came to create my mission, not only for my practice, but for Tina's Spiritual Circle, an open community of like-minded people bonding to each other with love. We pray, share, laugh, cry, heal, and connect to God in our own unique way without judging each other's differences in the way we make that spiritual connection. And this is the mission of *My Spirit Is Not Religious*™:

1. To enlighten you with spiritual insight that will help you achieve your highest purpose.
2. To assist your development of spirit and your alignment with peace, harmony, unity, clarity, prosperity, and enlightenment.
3. To inspire spiritual growth without limits.
4. To bring people together and create an enlightened community.

In Part I, I will help you recognize patterns that may have been ingrained in you from infancy—ideas and beliefs that can create havoc in your current life even though you may be unaware of them and their impact. I will share many religious stories of my own as well as those of people who have come to me for guidance. In Part II, I will help you come out of your "spiritual closet"—the private place where your own beliefs replace those with which you have been indoctrinated. You will learn how to embrace this hidden part of yourself. In Part III, I will give you the tools to tap into your spirituality as well as fight the inevitable guilt that can arise when you finally decide to strike out on your own path and abandon the faith of your family and friends. I will teach you how to further your spiritual journey. And in Part IV, I show you how to stay on spiritual task.

And all along the way, I will hold your hand and nurture your tender soul. I know this is a difficult transition as I have made it myself. But over the years I have helped thousands of people move toward their true selves and I know I can help you as well. You only have to take the first step. As Buddha tells us, "Just as a candle cannot burn without fire, men cannot live without a spiritual life."

Part One

A Different Way
to Feel God

Born Into
a Religion

All major religious traditions carry basically the same message; that is love, compassion and forgiveness. The important thing is they should be part of our daily lives.
—Dalai Lama

I was born into a religion, the Roman Catholic religion, to be specific. Now, I want to be clear that I'm not out to bash Catholics. My personal experience has been Catholicism, and I can use only my experiences as references. If you were brought up with a faith other than Catholicism, you will likely still find correlations between the faith in which you were raised and mine. As a result, you may relate to many, if not most, of my experiences.

I'm speaking of religion that does not work, religion that separates us from the Universe, the Divine, or what some people refer to as God. (For simplicity, I use the words God and Creator interchangeably, and I refer to God as male.) Whether this entity is female or male is unimportant especially in a conversation about religious beliefs that automatically define human beings as sinners. In law, as citizens we are innocent until proven guilty. In my religion and in most others, we are guilty until proven otherwise. I speak of religion that is hypocritical and inconsistent, religion that does not make common sense. religion that allows you to believe one way and act another. More often than not, this is known as organized religion.

You may experience the hypocrisy this way: you go to service/church, hearing from the pulpit that we are love, but so many fellow congregants then walk out the door with an attitude and energy of anything *but* love toward their friends, family, and neighbors. This experience seems to ricochet across belief systems; it doesn't matter whether you attend a church, temple, mosque, or synagogue. You may turn to religion for comfort but continue to find yourself wanting. Could this be because your religion is separating you from God, and you feel and see in your entire being that this is wrong? If that is the case, I urge you to move on.

"Easy for her to say," you might be thinking. "Moving on is easier said than done." I completely understand, my dear one, since I've been there. For as long as I can remember, I've always felt that religion was too confining, with too many rules, too much boxing in, too constricting, too judgmental – *and forget about fun.* Ever since I was a young girl, I remember noticing Catch-22 situations. I felt God, I saw miracles, I had faith, I felt my guides and angels. And then I saw people creating havoc in their lives, in their families, with their friends, in the environment, society, and country … it made no sense.

Throughout my life, organized religion was forced upon me by my parents, relatives, friends, nuns, priests, teachers, neighbors, and acquaintances. Amid it all, though, something was not sitting right in my being. I had a difficult time distinguishing what was right and what was wrong in every aspect of my surroundings. I was so confused. But I'd been taught to respect my elders, since they obviously knew best. . . .

My spirit felt caged in. I knew with my heart that religion was supposed to bring us comfort and love. It was supposed to be the place to find solace and express gratitude, a place of serenity, not a place of punishment. A place of joy and not sorrow. A place of harmony, not war. I couldn't abide by the fear of confessing sins to a non-nurturing stranger, or judging and condemning others because they didn't follow Jesus a particular way when I was taught that an all-loving Jesus would forgive and love everyone.

I, of course, did not express my views because I knew there would be grave consequences if I did. Instead, I went through the motions by rote, keeping my observations and beliefs to myself as I lived in my spiritual closet. This was a place of profound comfort, peace, and love. At any time, I could shut out anyone opposing *my* beliefs and choose to enter my virtual spiritual domain. The challenge was that no one else was allowed in because it was difficult to find anyone I could trust or who believed what I did. The result was that I was lonely, but safe, and I remained in my spiritual closet for quite some time.

||||||||||||||||||||||||||||||||||||||||||||||||||||||||

EXERCISE

In the "notes" pages at end of this chapter, list some beliefs you received from your experience with organized religion with which you no longer agree. What are some spiritual options that can replace the beliefs that no longer serve you?

Bonus: Download free exercises, meditations, tips, etc. at
www.TinaSacchi.com

||||||||||||||||||||||||||||||||||||||||||||||||||||||||

My Grandmother

I remember as a young child visiting my grandmother every year in Italy and watching her practice energy healing on others. People literally lined up at her door, waiting to see her all the time. Even at the young age of three, I knew in my heart that she was just going through the motions of attending church. I knew that if she'd only had the courage to stand up to the church and the culture within which it was so deeply ingrained, she would have been able to step out of her own spiritual closet and practice a less conventional spirituality of healing and energy that her own Roman Catholic Church would never have acknowledged or sanctioned.

But in a tiny town of 3,000 people, with more than enough rules to serve the entire Universe, my grandmother never considered letting people know how she really felt inside. Doing so would simply have been unsafe, for if her neighbors and friends had gotten wind of her beliefs, they would surely have seen it as opposition. They needed very little excuse to put heretics in jail and throw away the key. So my grandmother blended into society by attending every religious event, taking care not to ruffle any feathers. However, I know that if she'd had the opportunity, privilege, and security I've enjoyed to explore these issues, to guide others, and even to write this book, she would have taken it. Unfortunately, she did not. She lived at a time that was constrained and absurd. Spirituality became a secret, forced into the closet.

Growing Up in Brooklyn

I was born in Brooklyn, New York, in the 1960s, at a time of hope, freedom, exploration, and great change. I was part of the baby boom, hippies, flower power, peace, and love. In that era change was natural. Religion, on the other hand, had been the same for thousands of years; changes and updates in the beliefs, traditions, and teachings were rare.

We lived in a close-knit neighborhood. Everyone was either Italian or Orthodox Jewish, but it didn't matter which you were. A Catholic church sat at one end of the block, a synagogue at the other. The underlying reasons for participating in religion were the same. Segregation, guilt, and shame were the driving forces behind these religions, and they filtered down into our day-to-day lives. If you weren't Roman Catholic or Orthodox Jewish, no one would sell you a house or rent you an apartment in the neighborhood. People had to fit the mold. Polish, German, Puerto Rican, or whatever had to find their own neighborhoods. Was religion unifying us with other races, or separating us? The answer was becoming clear.

Make no mistake: I believe in a Higher Power. I believe there are things beyond Earth and my physical body. And I do believe I am a spiritual being having a physical experience, rather than a physical being having a spiritual experience. (If you don't see the distinction yet, you will.) But somehow my dissatisfaction and this incongruity between my real beliefs and the beliefs of seemingly everyone around me continued to grow. I attempted to delicately express my feelings to others, but their immediate reaction was always the same: *You don't really believe that, do you, Tina?* The implication was that there would be serious consequences if I did.

"What?!??!" I silently questioned. Does God really want to make our lives so difficult? Did God create this beautiful world only to have the beautiful people in it be constantly cranky, irritable, and judgmental? My heart and spirit were misaligned with everyone's strict obedience to Medieval rules to which I couldn't subscribe. So I kept my spiritual beliefs hidden. I went through the motions of attending religious functions when necessary, to appease my family, but I secretly practiced my own beliefs. I was the leader and sole follower of my own spiritual sect.

My parents, whom I love so dearly, literally got "off the boat" from a small town in Sicily, Italy – population 3,000 – and I was born one year later. Through the ages, many nations – the Romans, Vandals, Byzantines, and the Spanish, to name just a few – fought over the island of Sicily. The transformation of this island nation was great. Though Sicily experienced a "golden age" of multiculturalism and religious tolerance, it became predominantly Roman Catholic by the year 1500. Religion was very important to the nation, as faith kept the population together.

My parents were absolutely determined to pass their beliefs down to me. Their mission was to reinforce the religion that had been handed down for generations, whether or not it made any sense. This is what they knew, and without questioning any of it, they would do anything to keep their beliefs, traditions, and culture intact. They continued to carry religion through the generations, motivated by shame, guilt, and fear. Now, all was not wrong with this belief system. For one thing, I admire their determination. That is a quality I decided to take from my religious experience with my parents. It is this determination that brought me to write this book. But although one big positive emerged, many aspects of these religious beliefs still did not resonate with me.

Throughout my life, I had been abiding by many, many rules and regulations, quite a number of which related to religion. For one thing, I had to go to church every Sunday, although for some reason, God excused my father. He was the breadwinner of the house; he had to work erratic hours and was tired.

I attended a Catholic elementary school for 8 years, and then proceeded to an all-girls Catholic high school. Following that, I got my bachelors and masters degrees from a Christian university. For all those years, I lived in fear that if I didn't go to church or if I skipped confession, I would go to hell. Or that I would make a stop in purgatory (a place or condition of punishment due to sin) first and, after my time there, perhaps get the green light from God to go on to heaven. Down deep inside, I knew these were fanciful, untrue beliefs, but I was surrounded by so many people who really embraced these ideas as reality … or was it possible that they, too, were all putting up a façade out of fear of expressing themselves? Were others around me afraid to come out of their spiritual closets, too? They may well have been, but not knowing, I felt alone.

In The Confessional

During my childhood, confession was a must, once a week on Fridays. My friends and I would walk to church, discussing the week's sins. I would ask my girlfriend: "So what did you do wrong this week?"

"I lied to my mom and dad, and I cheated on my math test," I remember Ricki saying. "What about you?"

"I told my mom I was riding my bike on my block only, but instead I went off the block and rode to the schoolyard," I said. "If she found out, I'd be punished. Oh, and I also cursed a few times."

"How many times? You know the priest is going to ask you this."

"Yes, I know. Three times, I think." I sighed.

We walked up the church steps and into the gloomy, half-lit church. It was so quiet, with such an eerie feeling. No matter how often I had been inside that church, it still felt creepy every time I set foot in it.

"I wonder which priest we're going to get today," I mused. "I hope it's not the Monsignor. He is mean and slow and gives you a lot of prayers."

"Me too," Ricki agreed.

So here we were, at 10 years old, entering the church and noticing the other people lined up for their weekly cleansing from sin. We went to the back of the line, waiting our turn to enter the dark confessional box. This is not really a box so much as a closet that is divided into three stalls. The middle stall is where the priest enters, closes the door, and sits down on a bench. Attached to either side of the priest's stall is another stall with a curtain.

We would wait for the curtain to open, allowing the person who was in there to exit so the next in line could enter. Each outer stall also had a bench for the sinner to sit on. Inside each sinner's stall was a small-screened window, and a port door that the priest efficiently opened. He would listen to the recitation of sins and mete out the prayers for us to recite in church so that we could walk home, our souls cleansed for the week.

It was really dark inside the confessional box, and I could just barely make out the priest's conversation with the sinner on the other side. When he was done, I would hear a clunk, which signaled that the priest had closed the small port door to the opposite stall. It was my turn. I felt uneasy with all this drama unfolding. My hands would sweat and my heart raced. After all, I was only 10 years old, sitting in a dark closet waiting for the priest, the judge, to tell me I had sinned and bestow my penance, the prayers that would make everything all right again.

Confession was amazing to me. It didn't matter if I lied to my parents, stole candy from the store, or cursed. As soon as I said a few prayers, as directed by the priest, I was clear for another week. Wow. How could a priest – a mere human being – have so much power, yet I was not able to do this for myself? Without his help, was I really unworthy of true repentance, making peace, and moving on?

IIIIIIIIIIIIIIIIIIIIIIIIIIIIIIIIIIIIIIIIIIIIIIIIIIIIIIII

EXERCISE

In the "notes" pages at end of this chapter, record your religious story. Here are some questions to think about:

- Were you born into a religion or was it imposed on you by someone in another way?
- Did you receive formal religious education such as attending Sunday School, Catechism, or Hebrew School? How meaningful was this to your life?
- What was the importance of religion in your family of origin? Was it a central part of your upbringing? If so, how? If not, why not? How did that affect you?
- Describe what organized religion means to you.
- Which parts of your religion bring you closer to God? Which parts take you away from God?

If you were not born into a religion ...

- How does it feel to have grown up without one? Do you feel you were in some way deprived?
- What questions do you have regarding your parents or guardians and their beliefs about religion?
- If your parents or guardians were raised in a religious tradition and then abandoned it, why do you suppose they did so? How did their choice affect you?

Record your revelations from this exercise.

Bonus: Download free exercises, meditations, tips, etc. at
www.TinaSacchi.com

||||||||||||||||||||||||||||||||||||||||||||||||||||||

A Dark Time

As I got older and lived through many events and experiences, I began to discover that I was not alone in my challenges with my religion of birth. For instance, Steven, a successful businessman in his 30s, came to me a few years ago to see if I could do anything about his fear of the dark. He was a bit embarrassed to visit me about this problem, but it was getting worse and worse as time went on. He said he'd never had any problems, not even as a child. It was just in the past year that he would feel unsettled every evening. His anxiety and sleeplessness rendered him unable to focus on his previously successful business. All of this took a toll on his self-esteem, and he came in to see me feeling distraught.

"What changes have you experienced this past year, Steven?" I asked.

"Oh, nothing really out of the ordinary. Business has been consistently increasing for the past five years. Over the years, I have added a few sales reps, and they are all doing great. No dramatic changes," he explained.

"What about your relationships? Any changes there?" I asked.

"My wife Betty and kids are terrific. My boys are playing sports, and Betty is doing well with her floral business. Things are pretty much status quo," he reported.

"What about socially? Have there been any changes?"

"Well, not really. But I don't have the time I used to for getting together with my friends since I've gotten more involved with my boys and their activities. And with my business growing, it has also taken more time to train my sales reps," Steven added.

"Okay Steven. Is there anything you used to do that you're no longer doing?"

"Well, I really can't think of anything in particular, with the exception of the fact that I don't attend church anymore. My friends were all part of the church, and since I no longer go, I lost touch with them. I feel that church just doesn't do it for me. I used to be part of the money collection team on Sundays, raising money for the church. But, I was feeling so disconnected and out of place. It seems like my beliefs just evolved.

"You know, Tina," he continued, "I really feel more *religious* now – or should I say more *spiritual* now, than I ever felt before. All those years going to church, and I never got out of it what I'm now getting with my own practices of meditation and simply spending quality time with my wife and boys."

This gave me a good idea. "What beliefs were you taught about not going to church?" I pressed.

"Well, I was always told that if I missed church, I would go to hell. But I don't believe that anymore, Tina. I know we create our own hell, here on Earth. There is no place called hell. I know and believe that."

"I believe you, Steven," I said. "Now, when you were younger, what did you imagine hell to look and feel like?"

"I imagined it to be dark, gloomy, and full of evil spirits doing awful things to you, such as burning you with torches and slashing your flesh with different weapons," he explained.

"And how did it make you feel to imagine that?"

"Well, I felt scared and uncomfortable. It felt spooky. I remember making sure I attended church every week, since that thought frightened me so much."

"So how do those feelings and emotions differ from the feelings and emotions you're experiencing every evening as it grows dark?" I asked.

Steven sat up. "Oh, my gosh. They are exactly the same. Tina, I never made that connection. It's exactly the same. Oh, my. I never would have thought something I believed as a young boy could affect me now, when I should know better."

"So why do you think you're suddenly accessing this information from years ago?" I asked.

"It must have been embedded in my mind. It's a belief that was passed on to me, but I don't need to own it any more. It's not part of who I am now." Then he brightened. "How do I get rid of it?"

"Well, just having the awareness and connecting with it is a step in the right direction," I explained. "Many times, when we have awareness, we experience an immediate healing and resolution. I can also help you move the energy imprint out of your aura field, if you give me permission to do that healing for you."

"Yes, please. This is ridiculous. Let's do it." Steven said.

I proceeded to do just that, using various alternative healing techniques. When we finished, I asked that Steven come back in a month. He walked into my office the following month, proclaiming that I was a miracle worker. I thanked him for the compliment, explaining, however, that without his cooperation and permission, I would have not been successful.

"Yes, I know," Steven said. "But you tuned into the root of the issue. And by doing that, you helped me get to the root, which I was not able to do on my own. I thank you with my all my heart."

Notes

Chapter 2

The Other Limbo

**When I do good, I feel good; when I do bad,
I feel bad, and that is my religion.**
— Abraham Lincoln

C atholic doctrine states that thanks to the experience of Adam and Eve all humans are tainted by original sin. Baptism is essential for salvation. In the early centuries, it was declared that all unbaptized babies went to hell upon death. By the Middle Ages, the idea had softened to suggest a less severe fate. Although infants were too young to commit sins, unless they were baptized, they were not free of original sin. But instead of going to hell, they went to limbo, a place just on the edge of hell. Their souls would remain in limbo until God decided whether or not He would admit them into heaven.

However, a Vatican committee that spent years examining the medieval concept of limbo recently published a report reversing limbo's basic principle which is that unbaptized babies who die may not go to heaven. Never part of formal doctrine because it does not appear in Scripture, limbo was recently removed from the Church's teachings.

What happens to babies today who die before they are baptized? This question does not have a clear answer. But the concept of limbo and the decision to abolish it have had a profound impact. Can you imagine what happened during the centuries when people believed that unbaptized children went to limbo? I shudder to think about all those poor parents who'd had to live with the guilt and sadness that they should have baptized their children earlier. Because they believed their children's souls were in limbo, they had no doubt punished themselves, feeling responsible for causing their children so much pain since they had not been relieved of original sin. And now, after all those children had supposedly gone to limbo, it was declared that this state of being does not even exist? What are parents to believe? How are they to behave? And what of their years of self-criticism and their own suffering and guilt?

Another related belief concerns people who die before confessing their sins. They too would go to limbo. God would hold them in limbo until He decided that they'd paid their dues, at which time they would be relocated to heaven. Really? Well, what if someone died suddenly of a heart attack, stroke, or car accident and through no fault of their own were unable to confess before their death? Would they go to limbo too? What a concept. In fact, the idea of limbo has been rejected by many Catholics who see it as harsh and at odds with the actions of a merciful God. Think about it. Would an all-loving God put you in limbo because you were hit by a drunk driver? In my mind, this is nothing short of ridiculous.

Nevertheless, memories and experiences like these take up residence in our subconscious mind where all memories, experiences, and knowledge are stored. These sad memories play again and again throughout parents' lives, creating obstacles in their lives and causing remorse, guilt, sadness, disappointments, and fear.

Baptismal Crisis

Growing up in a strict Italian Catholic family, it was completely understood that as soon as a baby was born, you had weeks – if not sooner – to get that baby baptized. Come hell or high water, your top priority was to complete this religious task, pronto. When I was born, my mom wanted to wait for her father to come from Italy to be present at my baptism. He would arrive two months following my birth. Still, to this day, my mom tells the story with such drama and emotion, detailing all the grief she received from her family and friends. They all informed her that she would regret it if I died before I was baptized, that it was her motherly duty to get me baptized quickly. Every time my mother recounts this story, I think of the fear that shaped everyone's lives. These were emotions my mother lived with for two months while she was trying to nurture me as an infant. What a bunch of negative thoughts. How stressful. Why couldn't these people focus on the positive– that I was alive and healthy, and what a joyous occasion it would be when my grandfather arrived from Italy to meet me and celebrate my life?

|||||||||||||||||||||||||||||||||||||||||||||||||||||||||

POINTS OF REFLECTION

- Which beliefs and rules from your religion, though they have changed over time, are still running your body, mind, spirit, and emotions?

- Which beliefs and/or rules have changed for you? That is, you believed them at one time, but they no longer resonate with you?

Bonus: Download free exercises, meditations, tips, etc. at
www.TinaSacchi.com

|||||||||||||||||||||||||||||||||||||||||||||||||||||||

The Self-Blame Game

Lisa came to me in a deep depression. She filled out my standard intake form and indicated that she was anxious, depressed, lethargic, and sad most of the time, but she did not know why. She had even lost the will to live. The medications her doctor had prescribed had worked for a while, but eventually they'd lost their effect on her. She found it very difficult to get up and go to work or even to function. Attending church on Sundays was a big endeavor, although she gave herself all morning to get ready so she could participate in the 1 p.m. service.

First, I suggested to Lisa that she make an appointment with her medical doctor to see if her depression might have its root in a physical condition. But I then proceeded to ask if she had any idea why she had been feeling this way. Lisa claimed she had no clue. Intuitively, I felt it would be helpful to regress her with hypnotherapy. We called in her guides and angels, and I took her back to the first time she started having these feelings. It was a few months after she had suffered a stillbirth. The death came as an enormous shock, since all of her prenatal doctor visits had been perfect. But they could not prevent the tragedy that was to come: In the eighth month, Lisa's baby girl developed a clot in her umbilical cord that stopped the flow of blood and oxygen to her brain, and she died before she was born.

This is a tragic event for any family. The sudden loss of a healthy child at childbirth—a moment that should have been filled with promise and joy—turns into one of the most painful experiences parents, grandparents, and siblings can have. Lisa was no exception. She deeply felt the loss of her daughter and seemed unable to release herself from mourning. But her situation was complicated by old religious beliefs. In hypnotherapy, Lisa was able to make the connection between her daughter's death and her depression. But she also blamed herself for the fact that her daughter's stillbirth had caused the baby to enter limbo.

Lisa had been brought up in a very strict Catholic family. Her mother had changed her mind about becoming a nun when Lisa's grandfather fell ill and she found herself as his caregiver. Shortly thereafter, she met Lisa's dad. They married and had Lisa and her seven brothers and sisters. Lisa's mom strongly influenced her children with her religious doctrine. Lisa informed me that living in that family was just like living in a convent, with austere rules, regulations, bible study, and the like. Beliefs about purgatory, limbo, and heaven were second nature to her and her siblings.

Lisa had a hard time seeing any alternatives to her daughter being in limbo. So I asked her to define religion. She responded immediately, "Well, religion is serving God."

"How does one serve God?"

"Through love and understanding," Lisa responded. "Just like Jesus did. He loved everyone, in spite of their faults, beliefs, or creeds."

"So regardless of whether someone is at fault, we serve God by not punishing ourselves?" I asked.

"That's right," Lisa said

I pushed a bit further. "So if something is not our fault, we would not be held accountable, right?"

"Yeah, that's right," she answered.

"Okay, Lisa. So why are you punishing yourself? Why are you allowing this tragedy—the death of your unborn child—to be your fault? You are not serving God if you do this, are you?"

Lisa looked at me in bewilderment. Then I saw her eyes light up, and a tremendous, radiant smile quickly followed. "Wow ... I've never thought of it that way."

This was an incredible release for Lisa. She got in touch with her spirit, not the religion. The difference here was monumental, and something she had never done before. She realized that if she kept punishing herself, she would not be honoring her baby's soul. She discovered that she was one with God and not apart from Him. And if she was one with God, then her baby was too. In fact, they were all one. Once she stopped punishing herself and became compassionate and merciful toward herself, she was able to have a deeper connection with her lost baby. Energetically, I could see and feel her spirit lighten up. It was as if an immense burden had been lifted from her shoulders.

Notes

Notes

Chapter 3

Does Religion Unite or Divide?

**"There is only one religion, though
there are a hundred versions of it."**
—George Bernard Shaw

T he purpose of religion is to bring people together
to honor our Creator and make humanity as loving
as possible. Not long ago, I read the following on a
bumper sticker:

**Religion is for people afraid of going to hell.
Spirituality is for those who have been there.**

This made me ponder religion on a deeper level. Religion
was founded on the right intention, but it took a wrong turn
somewhere. The foundation is belief in a higher power, namely
God, and a focus on doing good works. Yet, I have found that
many religions use the mechanism of fear to encourage people

to think the same way, regardless of their inner knowing or belief. Fear is the opposite of love. So why does religion promote fear? The simple answer is that it allows those "in power" to control people. The dictionary describes fear as the likelihood of something unwelcome happening. In some religions, brainwashing occurs, causing everyone to go with the leader's flow, rather than with their own natural instinct, flow, and/or gut. In this way, institutionalized religion is used as a political or social force.

We are taught that we must love, but then we go out and judge, persecute, and kill others. We literally and figuratively stab others in the back. We gossip about our neighbors, friends, loved ones, and enemies. We segregate ourselves, building physical, mental, emotional, and spiritual walls and borders that disconnect us from each other. We say Jesus saves; however, we don't help save others. Throughout religion, lots of judgment takes place. Judgment is a form of negativity that tears us apart, rather than uniting us with our Creator. The result is that we are separated from God.

|||||||||||||||||||||||||||||||||||||||||||||||||||||

POINTS OF REFLECTION

- What does religion teach you about life?
- About relationships?
- About business?

Bonus: Download free exercises, meditations, tips, etc. at
www.*TinaSacchi*.com

|||||||||||||||||||||||||||||||||||||||||||||||||||||

Religion: A Different Sauce?

Clients and students often ask me, "Which is the right religion?"

Being Italian, I always respond with the same question: *"What kind of sauce do you put on your spaghetti?"*

And I always receive many different answers: alla vodka, bolognese, puttanesca, carbonara, marinara, vegetable, wine, and more.

Some people say "Marinara." And then I may ask, "Why Marinara?"

Most people say, "I just love simple, straight forward sauce without any fancy additions like cream, meat or veggies. Just plain old spaghetti and tomato sauce. The plainer the better."

Others may say, "Give me the works: tomatoes, veggies, meat and cream." Individuals have preferences they express in their own way. They are neither right nor wrong. Actually, it doesn't matter what type of sauce you prefer – ultimately we're still just talking about a spaghetti dinner. Right?

Apply this analogy to religion. Some people prefer to see their Creator as God; for others it's Adonai or Allah. The point is, it doesn't matter. Ultimately it's the Creator. It's your belief in a Higher Power that matters, not the nametag you put on him/her/it. What's important is that we connect with the Force to do good.

Some people worship in a church, others in a temple or synagogue or in a forest or on a mountaintop. Again, it doesn't matter where you worship; it matters that you worship with your heart and out of love.

A Different Way to Feel God

Religion is an expression of how you feel Spirit; we each have a different way to feel God. If you feel like marinara sauce and your friend feels like alfredo, your way is not necessarily the right way, but neither is your friend's. So when I say that my spirit is not religious, I mean that my spirit remains open to others' ways of expressing their relationship with God. I simply choose one way and they choose another. There is definitely room for both. Neither one is wrong or right. But I feel it's neither religious nor spiritual when people preach that their religion is the only way, and that all other ways are wrong. In that context, I can truly say that my spirit is not religious.

I have often found that the more rigid a religion is, the less open its members are to others' belief systems. And the less open people are, the more arguments, battles, and wars that result. Remember that God wants us to be united through love; he does not want us to destroy each other. Yet, all this religion continues to harm us in God's name.

Although there is much good to be found in religion, the negative rules drive me around the bend. Spirituality is **not** restrictive; it is loving. Love yourself unconditionally, and love others the same way, too. When this simple life plan is in place, no other rules and restrictions are needed.

I say start your own religion – that is, start your spirituality within, in your heart and at home.

Being a Gentile

In my mid-twenties, I finally met a wonderful guy whom I will call Howard. We got along in every way. We loved the same things and had the same interests. Our friends had fun with each other. We enjoyed each other's company and we laughed and joked all the time. It was a perfect situation. After years of searching and many relationships, it felt so refreshing to finally meet someone with whom I could be friends first, but also have the hope for a permanent relationship. Then, one day, Howard asked me a question:

"What is your faith, Tina?"

"I am Catholic," I said, swallowing slowly, with caution. Somehow, my spirit had known not to ask this question, but here it was, presented to me now. Innately I knew I wouldn't enjoy what was coming next.

"What about yours, Howard?" I asked.

I immediately saw the expression on his face go from happiness to complete sadness. "Jewish," he said.

I understood instantly the turmoil he was experiencing inside. You see, in the Jewish culture, the mother determines the children's religion. Consequently, it is very important for a man to marry a Jewish woman, or their children will not be considered Jewish. This is a vital aspect of the Jewish tradition with regard to passing on heritage and religion. However, in the more liberal branches of Judaism (practiced by the majority of American Jews), if a gentile woman converts, she is considered to be Jewish, and she and her children will be brought into the fold. But, there are some other elements that complicate matters. Since Judaism is a non-proselytizing religion, a prospective convert may be turned away three times before rabbis will accept to begin the conversion process. The woman needs to demonstrate with tenacity that she is truly committed to this new path. In addition, there are strong cultural issues. Even if a woman were to convert, her in-laws may not accept her or consider her "Jewish enough." She would still be thought of as an outsider because she had not grown up practicing the same traditions. Sadly, this was the case in Howard's family.

When I saw the look on his face, I sensed immediately what we were up against. "We can work this out, Howard," I quickly encouraged him. "We love each other so much."

"There is no way," he said. "My family insists that I date and marry a Jewish woman."

In that instant, I felt my heart break – but I was also angry. I felt not only discriminated against, but also a deep, deep wound. My emotions ran the gamut from feeling deprived and unworthy to feeling unloved, diseased, and worse. I was "just a Gentile," one of his friends had let slip one day. Here I had finally met a guy with whom I was totally compatible, and now he was telling me that Jewish laws written eons ago were dictating my life. Since I wasn't born Jewish…I was not good enough.

This reality was totally irrational and unreasonable to my being. What on Earth? "God," I screamed, "what are you doing to me, *now*? All my past relationships have been so challenging, and now you throw this curveball my way? Why are you *doing* this? It makes *no sense*. Especially not something that is *so simple* to work out. There is so much love between us – we can make it."

But we couldn't make it. The religious difference outweighed everything else. And Howard's reality didn't even take into account that my very Catholic parents would most likely have freaked out too. However I would have gone through with it.

I explained to Howard that it was time for him to take a stand in his life just as I would. And further, I asked him if it didn't sound completely absurd that his children – *our* children – would not be considered Jewish even though he was? "Besides, Howard, you never even go to Temple. You're not a *practicing* Jew." But there was no way out for him.

We went from being awesome friends who were together all the time to – the very next day – being out of touch with each other forever. I began a mourning process. My best friend was now totally gone from my life, all because of a nonsensical belief.

I started questioning religion. I started questioning its purpose. In retrospect, today I can honestly say that God set me up for an experience I never forgot, an experience filled with many different emotions. I went from being elated and joyous to feeling angry and disappointed. I learned a wide variety of emotions through one important life event. I often wonder what ever became of Howard. Is he finally living **his** life, or is he still living his family's? Is he happy? Does he have regrets? What would our lives have been together?

It's an understatement to say that experience was not fun. But honestly, I didn't understand then what I do now. Today, I thank God and my guardian angels for this outcome. I know my life would be totally different if I were trying to live up to the Jewish standards of a formerly Gentile woman living a Jewish life. It would not have been a life of complete joy, trying to convince my in-laws that I was worthy and capable as a mom, wife, and human being. And forget about living my passion as a spiritual teacher. That relationship with Howard was not in my destiny. My spirit nudged me to move on, and so I did. As a result, today I am so grateful for the way everything in my life has turned out.

We Are All Created Equal

Kamala came to me with a business dilemma and was looking for some spiritual coaching. She is a restaurant owner specializing in her ethnic cuisine: East Indian; she'd taken over the business from her parents who had run it for more than 35 years.

"How's business?" I asked

"It's great in spite of the economy," she said. "I am grateful for that. But what I need is guidance with my employees."

"What's going on?" I asked

"Well, I took over this business from my parents about five years ago. The thing is, they believe I need to employ all my family members and hire only people of the same race who follow the Sikh religion, like we do."

"Why do you suppose they believe that?" I asked

"'Because it's easier for us to understand each other,' they always say."

"So tell me about how your parents started this restaurant."

"They came straight from India and started to work in their relatives' restaurant. They worked hard and long for many years, saving money until they had enough to open their own place. They tried to keep the business authentic and helped their relatives and friends who came over from India by giving them jobs," Kamala explained.

"Are there still people coming from India needing these jobs?" I asked.

"Not really. Many of my relatives are finding their way in India."

"So who do they want you to hire now?"

"They want me to hire people of Indian descent," Kamala explained, "even if they are not related to us."

"And how is it working out with them?" I asked.

"Not good. I find that most of them will hop from restaurant to restaurant on a whim. They have no loyalty, even though I've done them – and my parents – a favor by hiring them."

"So who do you see working for you instead?"

"I know several people whose work ethic is outstanding and who are very in much in need of jobs – but they are not Indian," Kamala continued.

"Is it necessary for employees to speak the native languages at your restaurant?"

"Oh, no. Even the Indian employees who work there now are so far removed from their ethnicity that they speak fluent English. English is what's needed."

"Is it necessary for people to be of the Sikh religion to work at your restaurant?" I asked.

"No, not really, Tina. I must admit that I don't even follow it. I can't remember the last time I attended temple. It must have been years ago."

"So what you are telling me is that you have Indian people who look Indian; however, they don't speak the Indian dialects and perhaps may not even carry on the proper Indian religious traditions?"

"Yes," she said. "I think I see what you implying."

"What are some dominant beliefs that Sikhs hold?" I asked.

"To build a close, loving relationship with God, rejecting the caste system because we believe that everyone is equal," Kamala explained.

"So which religion do you follow now, if you haven't been to the temple in years?" I asked.

"I really do not attend any religious services. I pray and meditate every day, my own way of staying balanced and connected to God. I also practice yoga. That is what really works for me," Kamala said.

"Well, have you compared the rationale of hiring Indians today to the rationale your parents had for hiring Indians 35 years ago?" I asked.

"It's different." Kamala insisted. "The business has evolved; however the old beliefs remain."

"But if you're telling me that Sikhs believe everyone is equal, why would you discriminate in hiring employees?"

"Exactly." she said. "That is exactly it."

"And if you believe differently now, whose business are you trying to manage? Yours? Or your parents'?"

"Mine of course. I now see the whole picture, specifically that change has occurred, and that I must go with the flow of change. I feel confident now to stand my ground and try to make my parents understand how I see things. Thanks, Tina."

When Kamala followed up with me six months later, she told me that although her parents were not receptive to the idea of hiring non-Sikh Indians, she kept reminding them that their religious tradition was to treat everyone equally. Eventually, they softened and become more open to this change.

||||||||||||||||||||||||||||||||||||||||||||||||||||||

EXERCISE

- In the "notes" pages at end of this chapter, list the things religion has taught you that support your current beliefs.
- List the things religion has taught you that conflict with your current beliefs.
- How significant are the differences between your current beliefs and what your religion has taught you?
- If these differences are significant, ask yourself: "Is my religion truly serving me?" What makes sense and what makes no sense?
- What kinds of changes – in perspective or in practice – can you begin making so that your religious/spiritual beliefs are more congruent with your life?

Bonus: Download free exercises, meditations, tips, etc. at
www.TinaSacchi.com

||||||||||||||||||||||||||||||||||||||||||||||||||||||

Notes

Notes

Chapter 4
Beliefs, Myths, Truths, and Rules

Q: What weighs nothing and yet is powerful enough to start a war?
A: A belief.
— Contemporary Riddle

Opening My Eyes

Growing up in a neighborhood of Italians and Jews, I had a narrow view of the world. If we went on vacations, we would go to Italy to visit family in their town and come right back to our neighborhood. The view was still the same since my parents were adamant about raising me Italian and Catholic. I learned through those years that you either believed in Jesus and were Catholic, or you didn't believe in Jesus and were Jewish. In my neighborhood there weren't any other religions besides those two.

People did not relocate like they do today. Once you got married, you moved to a house, had kids, and most likely grew old and died there. We knew everyone on our block. Everyone knew us. We were also immersed in our community through the Catholic Church. Any activities I participated in were connected to the church. The Catholic schools I attended had clubs called Young Christian Students of which I was a member. I attended retreats following the same doctrine, rituals, and beliefs. The rules of our neighbors were all the same.

Looking back, everyone pretty much lived their lives similarly. We mimicked each other's ways and followed the prescribed rules and beliefs. The Internet wasn't popular for another 35 years in my world. Information wasn't readily available. So my view was narrow until I started traveling outside my cocoon.

My first trip without my parents was to Florida at age 17. My friend Julia and I hopped on a plane to a place that was so outside the box. This was exciting and yet I was anxious. We arrived at her aunt Helen and uncle Mark's place. Helen was a modern woman and so ahead of her time. She was divorced—something unheard of in my neighborhood—and now married to a man not only much older than her but of a different religion.

As we stayed there, I quietly observed their relationship and community. I realized the unbreakable rules that were so strictly enforced in my home and neighborhood were considered antiquated and ridiculous here. Throughout my stay in Florida, we interacted with Helen and Mark's friends and neighbors. I was like a sponge soaking in all that I discovered. Some things seemed so strange to me. Was I in a foreign country? No, I would remind myself. The plane ride was 2 ½ hours and went straight south and never left the USA. I had to pinch myself a few times. That trip opened my eyes to a bigger world.

I remember flying back and landing at JFK airport. I felt a closing in my heart. As we took a cab to our neighborhood, I looked at all the people walking to the market, sitting on their front stoops, doing the same things they'd done for decades. Do they not know there is a world out there outside of their rules? I realized then that my spirit needed more escapes from the old neighborhood so that I could discover my authentic spiritual self. I knew that there was more to life then following rules that I felt were so stultifying. I needed to explore. This moment of awakening began to shape how I viewed religion and then chose to live the rest of my life.

Beliefs, Myths, Truths, and Rules

I looked up some words in the dictionary and discovered the following:

Belief: Something one accepts as true or real; a firmly held opinion or conviction.

It said nothing to indicate that a belief at some point becomes a fact. However, millions of people around the world continue to fight over beliefs.

Myth: A widely held but false belief or idea; a misrepresentation of the truth.

Truth: A fact or belief accepted as true.

Rules: A law or principle describing or prescribing what is possible or allowable.

So looking at these definitions, we clearly see that myths, truths, rules, and beliefs are all created by humans. Actually, the leader or person in charge of any group ultimately dictates all of these. But if they are manmade, isn't that all the more reason to live according to *your* spirit, not anyone else's! Live your life according to your dreams.

Giving Up Bread

We have so many rituals attached to our religions, and often we repeat them without question—some of them for decades. Others, for centuries!

My Catholic upbringing was perfused with these rituals. Lent stands out in my mind. This is the forty days preceding Easter that is devoted to fasting, abstinence, and penitence. Forty days' worth of self-denial. Now if the objective of the fasting were our highest physical good, that is, to cleanse our bodies, I would say, let's rock on. However the connotation of this fasting is to suffer, just like Jesus suffered. Do you really think an all-loving being like Jesus would want us to suffer? Aren't we taught that he died for our sins, and by doing so eliminated our suffering permanently? Aren't we taught that he died to spare us even more suffering?

One common practice during Lent is to give up something you enjoy as a way of sacrificing and doing penance. Some people give up candy, TV, movies, smoking. In fact, we had to give up something during Lent, or else we were sinners. For many years, I gave up bread. I chose bread because I really love it, and the purpose of penitence and abstinence is to quit something you love. Let me tell you, bread is a difficult thing to relinquish. I eliminated toast, sandwiches, and dinner rolls from my diet for forty days. If you really enjoy eating bread, think about not having any for forty days—especially when others around you haven't imposed this restriction on themselves. It was no easy task!

What I didn't really understand was how relinquishing something I loved was supposed to make me a better person. Actually, it made me a little cranky. And if I was cranky, people around me got cranky, too. How was that a spiritual practice? My body was really missing an important dietary ingredient it needed to work efficiently. I didn't grasp the connection between suffering and being a better Christian. However, it was easier for me to just go along with the program and not question. So in order not to be a sinner, I gave up bread every year.

One day, after I had come out of the spiritual closet, Lent arrived and my family asked, "So, are you giving up bread again this year, Tina?" I hadn't even thought of it. I did not want to give up bread. What I wanted to do was nurture and feed my spirit, not diminish it and force it to suffer. I decided that feeding my spirit would make me a better person, a person who was with God, not apart from God. So I ate bread! I celebrated! I was happy. And everyone around me was happy. That is truly what God wants – happiness, not suffering.

Eating meat on Fridays or certain holy days of obligation is also a sin. We were committed to eating fish only. Now if you were sick, you were spared. Who the heck invented this rule? Who cares what you eat? What does eating certain types of food have to do with being a better Christian, or furthermore, a better person?

All these rules and obligations were not sitting well with me. I knew that God was not conditional. He did not create this world and the humans he made in the likeness of himself to destroy us in punishment, purgatory, or limbo. He also didn't intentionally create the world and then decide to make all of us miserable by imposing all these rules.

If we only spent more time celebrating life, loving ourselves and others, instead of playing these victim, martyr, suffering roles, then we would be living our spiritual lives.

We would be celebrating God with joy, not with resentment, disappointment, or self-abnegation.

Two Inches of Beef

An inspirational comedian I saw on TV a long time ago told a story that illustrates my point. One day she was preparing a roast to put it in the oven. She remembered her mom's recipe, so she seasoned the beef and cut one inch off both ends before putting the meat in the pan and placing it in the oven. She had done it this way for years, seasoning the meat, then cutting off the ends and throwing them away. One day, she thought about it. Why am I cutting the ends off this roast? It seems such a waste. So she decided to call her mom and asked her, "Mom, when you taught me how to make roast beef, why did you teach me to cut off the ends of the beef?"

Her mom laughed and replied, "Because that is what Grandma taught me. I really don't know why we cut off the ends. You're right – it is wasteful. Why don't you call up your Grandma and ask her?"

So the woman called Grandma and asked her, "Hey Gramm, why do we cut the ends off the beef before we put it in the oven?"

Her grandmother responded, "Well, I don't know why you two are doing that. The reason I cut off the ends was that my oven pan was too small. That was the only way the beef would fit into my pan!" She then added, "You're wasting food! Hasn't your mother taught you anything?"

This story clearly illustrates a process or ritual that had a valid origin. And there are lots of valid reasons for the things we do today. However, practices change over time. So, if it doesn't feel right, why continue? Change is inevitable. We must go with the flow.

||||||||||||||||||||||||||||||||||||||||||||||||||||||

EXERCISES

**Beliefs are not God. Feelings are God.
Religion is the fashionable substitute for belief.**
—Oscar Wilde, Irish dramatist, novelist, poet (1854-1900)

Which religious rituals, myths, or others' truths have you become accustomed to living, perhaps forgetting why you ever started? Have you ever considered whether they made sense to you?

_____

_____

_____

_____

_____

_____

List some of the habits you have created that no longer make sense, and what you can do to change them.

Bonus: Download free exercises, meditations, tips, etc. at
*www.**TinaSacchi**.com*

Routine religious practices	Why doesn't it make sense?	What can I do to change it?
I go to church every Sunday, regardless of whether I'm working a midnight-8 a.m. shift that day while my life is out of whack and I am tired exhausted.	Going home to sleep instead of going to church would make me feel connected, balanced and refreshed.	Take time out to connect to my spirituality and God in a different way – a way that creates harmony and peace in my life.

A. My True Beliefs	B. Beliefs I disagree with	Belief I can substitute for Option B
I love myself all the time.	I love myself only when I do the right thing.	I love myself all the time. I am human and I am continually learning.
I want to pray all the time.	Prayer is only effective if it's done in a holy building like a mosque or a church with a clergyperson leading the way.	God is within me, so the moment I start praying, I connect with the Divine.

Notes

Chapter 5

Lost in Translation

It is a fine thing to establish one's own religion in one's heart, not to be dependent on tradition and second-hand ideals. Life will seem to you, later, not a lesser, but a greater thing.
— D.H. Lawrence

aving been raised in religious schools my whole life, I have received instruction on religion and theology from many different teachers, each of whom had a slightly different perspective. Likewise, you can search the Internet and find many conflicts and discussions about which Bible is the most accurate.

The Bible is composed of 66 books, written by approximately 40 authors who were located in Asia, Africa, and Europe, over a 1,000- to 2,000-year span. At various periods in history, Jews and Christians agreed about which writings were inspired by God and thus authentic, and which were fake. And throughout the ages, Bibles have been translated by various committees with certain themes and purposes in mind.

Most of the bestselling Bibles are produced to create sales, so their translations are tailored to the masses. But by changing just a word or two, these translations can significantly alter the meaning of the message, and therefore impact sales. Furthermore, since no Bibles were written in English, much of its original message has been lost in translation. Being fluent in several languages, I know firsthand that when I translate a story from one language to another, the meaning is not exactly the same. People get the general idea; however, the authentic meaning cannot be fully captured or appreciated unless one is able to understand the story as it was originally written.

You may better appreciate this when you consider the area of the country in which you live. As a native New Yorker, I truly understand the meaning of a "New York minute." Having worked in the city for decades, I know full well all the intricacies involved with life there: a fast pace that's always moving with no time for standing still. Sure, I can explain to someone else what this means – but even though they may comprehend my description, they cannot fully appreciate the complexity of actually experiencing a New York minute or the hustle and bustle inferred from that phrase unless they've lived it, too.

I am not saying that the Bible is totally wrong. But I am saying that we need to use common sense in our daily lives. We can use the Bible as a guide; however, ultimate guidance comes from our spirit, from God. My spirit doesn't believe in killing in the name of God – that is an abhorrent idea. Yet many religious groups interpret the Bible as teaching this.

What's important is that we believe in God as a result of our free will. We believe in God because we feel him with our spirit, not because it was written long ago by someone else that we should believe, or because we've been told we "have to" believe or risk putting our souls at great peril.

There are easier paths to spirituality than reciting verbatim biblical passages that may or may not be an accurate representation of the original words.

Angels and Skeptics

A few years ago, while conducting a free seminar on a metaphysical topic in my community, the discussion moved toward angels and spiritual guides. I knew the moment I laid eyes on a man in the audience that he disagreed with my message. This man was not in any way forced to listen to me; he was there of his own free will.

Many of the audience participants had great questions and were eager to hear what I had to say. This man, however, heckled me continuously, asking questions such as, "How do you *know* there are angels?" And, "How do you *know* there are spiritual guides?"

I kept repeating one answer: "I know with my heart, sir." But the man was relentless. Finally, a group of audience members turned around and told him to be quiet. They had come to hear me, not him. At this time, I informed him that if he had any further questions or comments, I would answer at the end of the seminar. Surprisingly he stayed.

Sure enough, after I finished my presentation, he came over and asked me what book I was getting my information from. I informed him again that I simply feel the truth in my spirit.

He responded, "If the information you are teaching is not written in the Bible, it has to be false."

Honestly curious, I asked him, "Then why did you stay for the whole seminar if you don't believe in what I have to say? Why didn't you just walk out?"

His answer startled me: "You had interesting things to say."

So what's the point of this story? This man had been taught his whole life to believe that the Bible was the driving force of all truth. However, down deep inside, he was questioning this teaching. He resonated with the information I presented that evening. His spirit had guided him to stay and listen, with the hope that he might learn to become more open and flexible.

Warring Grandmas

Doreen came to see me with her eight-year-old daughter, Megan, who was having problems staying focused in school and did not want to attend church services at all.

I proceeded to talk with the young girl.

"So, Megan, what's going on in school? Your mom tells me you're having trouble paying attention to your teachers. Is that right?" I asked.

"They are all liars," she responded.

"Liars? That's pretty harsh. What are they lying about?"

"Everything! Nothing they say makes sense to me!" Megan exclaimed.

"Well, can you give me an example?"

"Yes! They tell me that Christopher Columbus discovered America. How do they know that? Who told them that?" she asked.

"Well, Megan, that is a fact, my dear. In 1492, Christopher Columbus and his crew landed on this continent and 'discovered' it," I tried to reassure her.

"Well, they are probably all lies," she continued. "Every book has different information, so I don't want to pay attention anymore."

"Can you tell me about the books that have different information?" I asked, gently.

"Yes! My Grandma Stein's book is different than my Grandma O'Leary's book," she said. "And they confuse me every time I talk to them."

"What book are you thinking about, Megan?"

"The Bible. Grandma O'Leary's Bible has more pages than Grandma Stein's. More stories. And Grandma Stein says those stories are not true. That's why her book doesn't have them," Megan said. "This makes me sad that my Grandma O'Leary is a liar. She is reading lies."

I was absolutely astonished. Each grandmother was attempting to pass on her religious beliefs to their grandchild, as if passing a religious baton. And each was extremely committed to achieving this. What an incredibly difficult situation for a child to experience. At the same time, I knew Megan was fortunate to be dealing with this issue now, at age 8, rather than suppressing it through the years and then needing to dig deeper to heal a bigger wound later in life.

At that point, I asked Megan to wait in the reception room while I talked with her mom.

"I can't believe what you're telling me," Doreen said. "It never dawned on me that our religions might be stirring up all this confusion for Megan. You know, when my husband and I got married, we promised each other that we would allow our children to eventually choose which religious path to take. We didn't want to influence them in any specific direction. I was brought up Catholic, and I am a strong believer, but my husband was brought up Jewish, and he feels just as strongly about his faith. I now see that this has put a tremendous strain on Megan. What can I do, Tina?"

"It's best that you and your husband openly discuss each other's beliefs, explaining to Megan that there are many different ways to think about God, but that one is not better than the other. Tell her it's up to her to choose the faith path her spirit believes in, and that you will both support her decision. And if she ever decides to switch to the other parent's belief – or something altogether different – you will always love her and are open and willing to talk with her about it.

"You may also want to consider talking with both grandmothers and asking for their support in this. It seems as if they're both very strong-minded in their positions. However, Megan is your child and she needs you and your husband to support her."

A few weeks later, Doreen brought her daughter in for a follow up visit. Megan told me she was listening and doing so much better in school. She also informed me that she had not decided which Bible was the right one. She planned to listen to both stories, and only then make up her mind.

I encouraged her to attend a kids' spirituality class I was teaching later that month so that she could learn to better listen to her spirit. She attended the class and became one of my youngest fans. The best part is that she is now connecting with her spirit and her heart.

||||||||||||||||||||||||||||||||||||||||||||||||||||||||

EXERCISES

The Bible tells us to love our neighbors, and also to love our enemies; probably because they are generally the same people.
— G. K. Chesterton (British writer and lecturer, 1874-1936)

Have you ever quoted the Holy Books like the Bible, scriptures, etc. to anyone? If yes, to whom, and under what circumstance?

_____

_____

_____

_____

How do the teachings of the Bible and other Holy Books affect or guide your life? Do you attempt to live by this book, regardless of whether doing so goes against your gut?

_____

_____

_____

_____

Is your belief in your Holy Book one of cultural knowledge, your spiritual truth, or a combination of both? Is your cultural and traditional upbringing affecting your spirituality? Explain.

_____

_____

_____

_____

In general, how well do you think most people live up to your Holy Book's teachings and scriptures? Do you believe people are doing the best they can in living a spiritual life? Explain

_____

_____

_____

_____

||||||||||||||||||||||||||||||||||||||||||||||||||||||||

Bonus: Download free exercises, meditations, tips, etc. at
*www.**TinaSacchi**.com*

Notes

Chapter 6

Who Is God and What Does He Want?

When you speak from your heart, everyone listens – because God is talking.
—Author unknown

God, the creator of the Universe, has countless names, perhaps because we cannot come up with one to encompass all that He or She represents: the Great Spirit, the Creator, Higher Power, Lord, the Almighty, the Maker, the Father, the Godhead, Jehovah, Yahweh, Brahma, Allah, the Universe, and even the Man Upstairs, to name just a few. But God is more than this. We are God – all of us equal God.

So who is God? Well, the answer to that depends on how you view God. If you view Him as separate from you, then you probably think of Him as a ruler, the almighty being sitting on his throne, waiting to reward or punish us for our deeds. A being who plays games with us. A being who is not really invested in whether we are sad or happy. A being who, on a whim, will allow us to suffer – or, perhaps if he is in a benevolent mood, toss us a bone so we feel lucky.

Alternately, if we view humanity as part of God, then we know that God is all-loving and is on our side. He wants to see us succeed in loving ourselves unconditionally so that we can love others unconditionally, as well.

We *are* all connected. We are all *one*! When you look into another's eyes, you are looking at God!

Want something more tangible to back this up? How many times have you been thinking of someone and then received a phone call from that very person? What's the first thing you say to them? "I was just talking about you!"

Or how about those times when you feel something is wrong with a loved one, so you call, only to find out that your intuition was accurate?

The reason these things happen is that we are energy, and as such, we read and pick up on others' energy through our senses. Since we are all connected, we sense what others are thinking, saying, and feeling.

I like to use the illustration of a Ferris wheel, which has a hub, and connected to the hub are spokes. Well, if you think about it, God is like a hub, and we are all the spokes. Because we are connected, we have direct access to God through prayer and meditation.

Now, Ferris wheels require mandatory safety inspections, mechanical checks, scheduled parts replacement, and lots of lubrication. Dust in the environment needs to be eliminated. And the main support bearings at the center of the hub require regular greasing and cleaning. Thus the analogy continues. Human beings also require routine maintenance, clearings, and healings of our physical bodies. For if we neglect any aspect of maintenance – body, mind, emotions, or spirit – we lose our connection to God and we lose sight of our purpose.

Since we are connected to the hub, we are in constant contact with it. Should our spoke become disconnected, we lose sight of our purpose and journey. We lose the love, instead becoming judgmental and envious and hateful. All it takes is one spoke – that is, one person – to disconnect, and the rotation of the entire wheel is affected. The cars attached to the wheel become inoperable, and in short order, the whole wheel runs off kilter.

The bottom line is that we must all come together and be love, be the light, be with God. We must join for the purpose of manifesting the Divine plan. In doing so, our God/human Ferris wheel remains in working order, turning smoothly, the hub and spokes working in perfect harmony.

To Nun or Not To Nun?

While I attended Catholic elementary school, God was really close and dear to my heart. I remember that in the sixth grade, I had the intention of becoming a nun. My innate thoughts and feelings told me that I wanted to be closer to God, and becoming a nun seemed the perfect way to do so. With nuns all around me, I seriously considered pursuing that vocation.

However, I also had a very strong feeling that there was something else for me—something else instead of the confinement of Catholic Sisterhood which would touch only a small group of people. I was looking for a way to reach out to more people from different spiritual backgrounds in addition to Catholics. I didn't know how it would happen and was not really sure how to proceed. And so I went with the flow. In a natural progression I went from a Catholic elementary school to an all-girls Catholic high school. As the years went by, becoming a nun faded from my dreams. I was a little distraught by this, though, since I didn't know at that time of any other ways to get closer to God.

Soon, though, my metaphysical beliefs started overtaking my religious beliefs, even though I kept these ideas hidden. At the time, I belonged to the Young Christian Students youth group. One of the members told me that the best way to get close to God was by becoming a nun or a priest. As soon as Kathy said that, I realized just how suffocating that idea was. I knew that God would definitely allow others to be just as close to Him; one did not need to become a nun or a priest. There were other ways.

So I challenged Kathy by asking more questions. It was her last statement that really changed my entire perspective. "People who attend church and parochial (Catholic) schools are somewhat close to God, but nuns and priests are automatically much, much closer to him.

"Whoa!" I thought, "That is small-minded." I went home and looked up the word "parochial" in the dictionary and it said: *having a limited or narrow outlook or scope*. That did it for me. I completely gave up on the idea of becoming a nun. What a relief! However, now I had no idea how to serve God. So I asked myself a question: ***What does God want?***

I put myself in His place and tried to think from His perspective. I also tried to feel from His perspective. I felt that He wanted us to unconditionally love ourselves and others. This made me feel much better. So going forward, I focused on love because ***that*** is what God wants!

Serving God Your Own Way

Charles came to me a few years ago with strong feelings of not belonging. He was 22 at the time, and had grown up in a religious family of eight children. The entire family attended services regularly. As a matter of fact, they had received assistance from their church for many years. His father's salary was inadequate to support eight kids. As a result of this financial aid, the family had dedicated a lot of time to various activities and functions at their church. Nevertheless, Charles explained to me that he found the religious services boring and that he disagreed with many of the church's teachings and beliefs.

"What is the mission of your church?" I asked him.

Charles thought about it for a while and finally responded, "To believe in God and love others like you love yourself."

"Well, do you believe in God and love yourself, Charles?" I asked

"Oh, yes. I do," he said.

"What about loving others? Do you love others?" I asked

"Well, I don't know, because if I don't attend my religious services, my parents are going to think I don't love them," he said. "And I probably wouldn't be loving my fellow members, either."

"So what kind of love do you have for someone if you're showing up half-heartedly?"

"Gee, I really don't know," Charles answered.

"OK, let's come back to this a little later. Let me ask you, what do you do as a service to others that you thoroughly enjoy?"

"Well, I love raising money for various organizations I believe in by running in marathons. I try to be involved in a race every month," Charles said.

"So you are making an impact in a different way than the way your family members are serving God. It may not be directly through your church, but you are definitely making an impact. With all your activities, the awareness you are bringing to wonderful causes, and your loving energy, do you really think you're not part of the big picture? I think God is very impressed and proud of your accomplishments. You truly demonstrate someone who loves himself and loves others through his actions."

Charles' face brightened. "Hey, that makes total sense! I never thought about it that way. I always thought I had to serve God every Sunday. But I am serving Him in my own way. That's great. Thanks, Tina!"

||||||||||||||||||||||||||||||||||||||||||||||||||||||||

EXERCISES
Give up the idea that God has a penis, unless she does.
—Author unknown

Who is God to you? Does God have a gender? Do you call him/her by a different name?

_____

_____

_____

Do you feel that God is a part of you or do you feel that s/he is apart from you? If you feel apart from God, what are some things you could do to feel more connected?

_____

_____

_____

Is your idea of serving God connected only to church and religious activities? Is that satisfying to you? If not, in which other ways do you/can you serve God?

_____

_____

_____

||||||||||||||||||||||||||||||||||||||||||||||||||||

Bonus: Download free exercises, meditations, tips, etc. at
*www.**TinaSacchi**.com*

Notes

Chapter 7

How Does God Communicate With Us?

**A man came to a guru and challenged him:
"I will give you an orange if you can show me where God is."
The guru answered:
"I will give you two oranges if
you can show me where God is not."**
—Source Unknown

*I*f you believe we are apart from God, your view is different than if you believe we are part of God. I resonate with the latter belief. I believe that as God, we are all interconnected and interrelated. Before we came to Earth, we were with God; just because we became earthlings doesn't mean that we became disconnected from our connection and communication with Him.

We all receive messages from the Great Spirit in many different ways ... through our senses, animals, nature, people, angels, spiritual guides, and more. We would probably prefer to receive these messages through modern human communication channels like phone calls, email, or even snail mail; however, we must learn to discern these alternate message delivery systems.

This point reminds me of an old joke. A man escaped from a cataclysmic flood by climbing onto his roof. There, he prayed to God for help as the waters rose. Soon a horse swam by and asked him if he wanted a ride out of the water. But the man said, "No, God will provide." And he stayed on the roof as the water continued rising. Then some men rowed by in a canoe and asked him if he needed help and he repeated, "No, God will provide." So they went on. Finally, the water swallowed him up and he drowned. When he got to heaven, he was angry at God. "Why didn't you come when I called you? Why did you let me drown?" he asked.

And God said, "Well, I sent you the horse and the men and the boat. . ."

A Stranger on the Road

When I was 25 years old, even though I was only a beginning skier, I decided to take a ski trip to Austria with a few friends. That is, I had been skiing perhaps three times, and the "bunny" slopes were the only trails I knew. We discussed the trip with just a handful of friends, but as often happens, you tell one person about something, and that person tells another, who tells someone else, and so on. Fifty-seven people wound up going on this trip! The airplane was practically our private jet! What fun!

I was so excited about the vacation. Our group came from many different backgrounds: students to corporate types to secret service agents to blue collar workers. With people of such diverse experience, I felt in my heart we were going to have quite an adventure.

We arrived in Austria and soon were skiing in the Alps! What magnificence, what beauty! "Wow, God. You really know how to create grandeur and glorious masterpieces, with trees, soil, snow, and stones. Words cannot describe the splendor of these mountains, of this place. Amazing!"

Our first day, we all skied together, focusing on one specific area of the mountains. This was rather easy for me. The second day, we got to the top of St. Anton and five of us decided to break off from the rest of the group so we could try a different trail. If you're familiar with skiing in the United States as compared to European skiing, you would know that the trails in the U.S. are clearly marked. As a result, you are confident that if you take a specific trail, it will lead you to the bottom of the mountain where a chair lift, ski lodge, and hot chocolate are waiting. Skiing in the Alps, however, is altogether different. There aren't any clearly marked trails, so you really need to know what you're doing. I overheard someone say, "If you're going to go off by yourselves, you may want to hire a ski guide to take you." We probably should have heeded that advice!

But I was all set to have an adventure, remember? So the five of us took off without a guide, thinking we were heading down a trail marked for skiing. Guess what! We were going *off the trail*. We ended up in an area of the forest where the snow was several feet deep. Shortly, the snowy surface became a layer of thin ice! So there we were with skis, poles, wearing weighty clothing and heavy boots; we kept cracking the ice and breaking through, continuously sinking into the snow! Every time we sank into the snow, it felt as if we were sinking into quicksand.

At that point we removed our skis, sliding them across the ice in front of us, hoping they would not break the ice and sink. We would also delicately throw our ski poles forward. Then we'd try to get out of the snow and move forward, toward our equipment. It took forever for us to move just a few feet. We were exhausted and frightened; thoughts of dying even crossed across our minds. We struggled to find any kind of level plateau where we could recuperate and catch our breaths. We had a few snacks with us, but that was all. Hours passed, and we finally reached a place in the wilderness where we were able to regroup.

The first thing we did was pray.

No one was around. We couldn't hear any voices or any sounds except the stillness of the mountains. We had no idea where we were, but we let our intuition guide us, knowing we needed only to move forward and head down the mountain, following gravity. Thank God at this point the surface was solid enough to allow us to ski.

We came upon a curved road along the edge of the mountain. Although no cars or buildings were in sight, we waited awhile, hoping a vehicle of some kind would show up. But this was an untraveled road, and we knew we needed to move on before it got dark.

Just as we were getting ready to leave, we saw a man walking toward us along the road. This was definitely odd. We were in the wilderness, and this person was on foot! He came right over to us and asked how he could help us. He even spoke English! We told him we needed to get to the St. Anton Ski Lodge. He informed us that we were way off course, but if we would travel in the direction he was pointing toward, keeping the sun always at a specific place in the sky, we would get there.

We were so grateful! The five of us thanked him profusely and headed off. When I turned around to wave goodbye, he was gone! Where could he possibly have gone? To this day, I know in my heart that God answered our prayers and saved us from catastrophe.

We did exactly what the man told us, heading in the direction he had pointed. We came across a few towns and each time, we reminded ourselves of our day and how grateful we were for that man. In answer to our prayers, God had brought him to us to nudge us back on track. We finally arrived at our destination, feeling relieved, safe, warm, and touched by grace.

Snakes, Hummingbirds, and Armadillos, Oh My!

Though my Alps experience was profound and unusual, we all receive messages from God. Remember, we are all one and we are all connected. If we believe that God is omnipresent—present in all places at all times—then we know God exists in stones, plants, and animals. In fact, many of my clients have shared stories about receiving messages from God through animals. What follows are some of them:

Bill and the Snake Skins

"I had been trying for years to get rid of old relationships and behaviors. Year after year, I would repeat the same relationship with my girlfriend. We would get together and then break up, over and over again. You indicated in a phone reading that it was time for me to move on. My spirit, mind, and body could not take this roller coaster anymore, and I needed to take the lessons I'd learned and let go completely.

"I had been very worried about how to manage this breakup, when suddenly I began to notice more snake skins on my ranch than usual. And I remember what you told me to do. 'Bill, just let go like the snake, in one big swoop. The snake sheds its skin in one piece, without reservation and without attachments. The snake never looks back with regrets or remorse – it just moves forward.'

"Thanks, Tina, for the great messenger that you are. I'm moving on ... sssssssss!"

Penny and the Hummingbird

"I just wanted to share my experience with a hummingbird today. I was having a horrible morning at work – I was so frustrated and stressed out that I was close to tears. I was called into the financial advisor's office – who happened to be one of the people driving me crazy – to receive more projects/problems to work on. I felt like I was at my breaking point and just needed to walk away from my job.

"Right at that moment, I looked out the window and saw a hummingbird flying all around, right up against the 9th floor window! I smiled and laughed at the way this little bird was flying so fast and crazy. I realized I needed to take a breath and calm down, because I was running around fast and crazy too, just like the hummingbird. In that instant, I realized nothing was worth getting so stressed out and upset about. I needed to roll with the punches, rather than getting caught up in everyone else's chaos and stress.

"Thanks, hummingbird, for showing me how crazy I was acting and feeling!!"

Sonia and the Armadillo

"Because I'd been having problems saying no to family and friends, my house had truly become a revolving door. Everyone came by whenever they felt like it. I used to thrive on this type of interaction; however, I was beginning to get stressed out with so many people invading my space. For months, I'd been praying to God about what I should do, but I didn't seem to be getting any response.

"Then a few months ago, I noticed that several different armadillos had been visiting me in my backyard. Armadillos are not unusual in Florida. However, I was seeing them consistently. During my phone reading with you the other day, you enlightened me about what armadillos mean. They simply go within, so that no one else can enter. For me, they were an indicator that I need to create boundaries!

"And Tina, you informed me that I can create boundaries with love that people will respect. While some may not understand it at first, over time they will appreciate my need for them to respect my space. This has been God's answer all along. I guess I was just expecting it to come in different way.

"Thanks, Tina, for enlightening me and guiding me to the answer."

||||||||||||||||||||||||||||||||||||||||||||||||||||

EXERCISES
There are no words to explain the unexplainable.
— Author unknown

Is it possible that God has been trying to communicate with you but you didn't know how to listen or what to listen to? If so, write about these missed opportunities.

_____

_____

_____

List some of the different ways God has communicated with you.

_____

_____

_____

_____

How has God answered your prayers? Were the answers direct, or did they come in unexpected ways?

_____

_____

_____

_____

Bonus: Download free exercises, meditations, tips, etc. at
*www.**TinaSacchi**.com*

||||||||||||||||||||||||||||||||||||||||||||||||||

Notes

Chapter 8

Love Is Love
Is Love

**We've got this gift of love, but love is like a
precious plant. You've got to keep watering it.
You've got to really look after it and nurture it.**
—John Lennon

The oneness and unity of all life is a basic principle
of spirituality. Oneness is the foundation of the new
spirituality: we are all one.

As humans, we all do the same things. We get up in the
morning, pee, and poop the same way. We eat several meals
throughout the day, make a living so we can pay our expenses,
create social interactions, and share concerns about our
health, relationships, family, and friends. Regardless of how
"different" we are, we all pretty much go about our days in
similar ways. One thing we all desire is to love and be loved,
and it is up to each of us to choose whom to love.

Love is love is love. As long as there is love, does it really matter if two women are loving each other, two men, or a man/woman combo? Does it matter if the partners are of different colors? Different shapes? Sizes? Flavors?

I count several homosexual couples among my friends, and I witness so much love and caring between them ... often more than the heterosexual couples whom I know express to one another. Their respect and honor for each other is outstanding. The caring and admiration between them is sensational. Some of my heterosexual friends yearn to have this type of fulfilling relationship, and yet some people continue to denounce this love! They have the audacity to claim it a sin.

If God does not denounce this love, why should we humans take it upon ourselves to do so? If there is love between a couple – regardless of their sexual preference, age, color, or creed – who cares?

Not Italian Enough

I was expected to date only Catholics – Italian white guys, to be specific. That was a strict demand placed on me. The thing is, the more my parents and family insisted on this rule, the more interesting I found "the others" to be. During my dating years, I went out with my lost love Howard as well as many other non-Italian guys. As a matter of fact, if I discovered a guy was Italian, I would almost invariably choose not to see him. I met all sorts of guys from different ethnic and religious backgrounds, and in doing so, I learned a lot, including that their families wanted their sons to date and marry girls of the same ethnicity and religious background too. Mine wasn't the only family that believed this way.

Finally I eased up on my family's restrictions about dating non-Italians. I was open to everyone – *including* white, Catholic, Italian guys. My experiment was over ... or so I thought. The funny thing I discovered was that there were sub-rules: it wasn't enough for the guys to simply be white, Italian, and Catholic.

One day, my Uncle Pete asked me about my boyfriend, "So what is he?"

"Italian," I answered.

"Good, Tina. Finally you are coming to your senses," he said.

I smiled, knowing he felt I was headed in the "right" direction, according to his standards.

"So what kind of Italian is he?" Uncle Pete continued the interrogation.

"Napolitano," I said. (*Napolitanos are people from Naples, Italy.*)

"No good!" he said. "Dump him!"

"But why, Uncle Pete?" I asked.

"You've got to marry a Sicilian and only a Sicilian," he said loudly, clearly disgusted.

Now, I could have battled him on this point, but I knew it would get me nowhere. No one was good enough, according to his way of thinking. Even if my boyfriend's family had come from the same town in Sicily as our family, from the same street in that Sicilian town, it would never be good enough.

So I said, "Uncle Pete, I am happy. Will you please find it in your heart to feel happy for me right now?"

He shook his head and left the house, mumbling under his breath.

From this experience, I learned that the only one who can make me happy is me. It would be a waste of my life to try to make others happy, so I decided to go for love in my relationship. Race, religion, political persuasion, color, ethnicity, national or social origin, sexual orientation, marital status, physical or mental disability didn't matter! I was going to live my life according to my spirit, not anyone else's beliefs, judgments, or opinions. This is my life!

Living a Lie

Dina, one of my high school girlfriends started dating a guy named Marco. They got along famously. They did many things together, and I could tell they had so much fun with each other. Every time I saw them, I sensed the closeness and respect they had for one another.

Both Dina and Marco came from huge, close-knit Italian families where there's a rule that if you date a girl for a long time, the next obvious step is marriage, or you will never hear the end of it. After six years of dating, Marco popped the question, and they got married.

Dina and Marco had the traditional wedding production with a fancy wedding hall, live music, sit-down dinner, bridal party, limousines, etc. But as soon as they were married, Marco started to act out and change his behavior. He would come home late every night; sometimes Dina didn't even know where he went after work. He would just tell her it was none of her business.

This went on for several months until one day Dina received a phone call from a person Marco had been seeing, who disclosed everything to her. From this caller, Dina learned that Marco was gay! The man who called was his lover. Dina was in shock. How could she possibly have missed this? Why had she not seen the signs? She started to blame herself. Where had she gone wrong? Was it her fault that Marco was gay?

Being close to both of them, I learned about both sides of this experience. Marco had known that he was gay for his whole life; however, coming from a strict, intolerant family, he knew he would have been exiled if he'd ever divulged his sexual orientation. He loved Dina completely as a friend, and that is exactly what they had been all those years—friends. After they married, though, he began working late in order to escape the sexual intimacy he knew would be expected of him. This then nudged him to follow his spirit and heart. He started to frequent places where like-minded people congregated, which is how he met his boyfriend. But he was seriously conflicted about how to break the news to Dina. So his boyfriend did it for him.

Dina, on the other hand, was totally blindsided. Coming from a strict Italian family where she abided by the rule that sex was saved until after the wedding, she had no clue about Marco's sexuality, or even her own. She was a virgin when they married. She had felt so close to him and knew only that they got along famously. Dina was devastated. And she was furious at Marco for not living his truth and causing her heartache because of it.

Marco had caved in to the family pressure that being gay was unacceptable, and that to reveal it would have meant being disowned. So he lived thinking that maybe one day, his gayness would go away. That if he married in a church with plenty of hope and faith, things would change and his life would be "normal." The church had taught him to believe in miracles. It was possible, then, that if he married, a miracle would occur to transform him from a gay man to a straight man … wasn't it?

What a tragic situation for both of my friends. Had Marco been allowed to follow his spirit and heart from day one, he would not have experienced any expectations about his relationship with Dina. They would have just been friends, and Dina would have been free to look for love and a husband elsewhere. But as it turned out, miracles did happen for both Dina and Marco. After many lessons were learned for everyone through this experience, Marco relocated to another state. He is happy living his life as an openly gay man while Dina remarried and now has a beautiful family and a dedicated husband.

The bottom line is that love is love is love. Just love and follow your heart because your heart always knows.

|||||||||||||||||||||||||||||||||||||||||||||||||||

EXERCISES

When we're free to love anyone we choose,
When this worlds big enough for all different views,
When we're all free to worship from our own kind of pew,
Then we shall be free.
—Garth Brooks, American country western artist

Has a parent, guardian or anyone imposed on you whom to love? If yes, what did you do? What did you learn?

_____

_____

_____

_____

_____

If you allowed a parent or guardian make a decision for you, what would you do differently if you had to make the decision yourself?

_____

_____

_____

_____

_____

What types of feelings and emotions have these decisions created in you? Do these feelings and emotions serve you?

_____

_____

_____

_____

If these feelings and emotions do not serve you, what could you do to begin creating new beliefs that do serve your spirit?

_____

_____

_____

_____

Notes

Part Two

To Come Out or Stay Inside the Spiritual Closet

Chapter 9

Are You Wasting Your Soul?

If you don't use your spirit, someone else will.
—Tina Sacchi

*Y*our belief is that your spirit has a specific mission here on Earth ... otherwise you wouldn't be reading this book. Your spirit's mission is to live out its purpose, which includes loving yourself and others unconditionally. But if you keep following the same wavelength you've been traveling since you were introduced to the restrictive beliefs of your religion, you will remain in the spiritual closet. If you stay in your closet, your spiritual purpose most likely will go unfulfilled and you will always have that question eating at you: Am I doing what I came to Earth to do?

At your deathbed, you will have one thing to justify to yourself and no one else: How could I have allowed myself not to fulfill my spiritual purpose? How could I have allowed myself live such an unhappy life?

So my question to you is this: Are you ready to die?

Whose Dream Are You Fulfilling?

Growing up, I always wanted to follow in my grandmother's footsteps by becoming a holistic healer. I watched her facilitate so many healings – people would literally line up at the door, waiting for her hands and prayers. However, my parents were adamant that I get a college education and work in an office "like the other well-paid, educated professionals are doing," they would say. Neither of them had the privilege of attending high school or college. As a matter of fact, I would be the first on both sides of the family to fulfill that dream.

Every time I mentioned wanting to go in another direction, they played the money card. If I chose a different route and didn't go to college, they would not help me financially; I would have to pay my own bills toward the household immediately. Thinking about this at age 17 was a bit scary for me, so I enrolled in college and chose Finance as my major. After all, if you learned finance, you could learn how to make it financially.

So I got my MBA and worked in Corporate America for almost two decades. I climbed that ladder to success in executive positions, even becoming a business professor at a local college. I got all the way to the top, and found myself wondering, "Is this it? Is this what I've been working 60- to 80-hour weeks for?"

Suddenly, I began feeling ill; I developed arthritis, diabetes, high blood pressure, shingles, and weight, gastric, and digestive problems. I was too young to have all of these ailments—only in my early 30's! Was this how it was supposed to be? I felt so disconnected. Deep down inside, I knew there **had to be** something better than this. I wasn't living my dream, my purpose. I was living my parents' dream.

But what **was** my dream and purpose? I only knew I wasn't on my journey toward it – if I had been, I would not have been ill and distraught.

A Turning Point

In 1996, I witnessed a miracle: the birth of my first son. I connected to him in such a deep, profound way. Not only did a sperm and egg get together when fertilization took place, but a spiritual being was created and born. The spiritual connection I had with my son, Joseph, was so amazing, so deep, and so extraordinary. It was one of the best days in my life!

I felt that if God was all loving – and he/she had to be to assist me in creating this miracle – why would he or she ever send me or my offspring to hell? Or to Purgatory? Or even Limbo? These old-fashioned beliefs from my family definitely were not my truth. I decided to be strong and follow my knowing, my heart, and my spirit. I drew the power from within me to protect this life I had helped bring into the world. And I started questioning everything on an intense level.

I was still in my spiritual closet, but that didn't stop me in my endeavors. I meditated regularly, and my guides clearly explained to me that it was better to keep my commitment to my purpose, which does not depend on other people keeping theirs.

I decided to give up my career in finance to raise my son. I wanted to witness this creation of mine and be part of his daily life. That was a turning point for me. While away from corporate America, I began an intense study of all things metaphysical ... still in my spiritual closet, of course. Very rarely did I tell my family or friends what I was reading or share my interests with them. I walked on eggshells and filtered each situation to determine whether it was acceptable to let particular people know what I was doing. Even my husband was on the fence regarding my new studies and beliefs. I felt incredibly alone.

Once in a while, I would delicately and cautiously ask my friends what they thought of reincarnation or whether they thought it was possible there was no hell … and I consistently received answers that were incongruent with my beliefs. So I secretly enhanced my holistic and metaphysical skills so that no one would burst my spiritual bubble! I was going to follow my spirit, even if I had to do it alone. I was not ready for judgment, segregation, or isolation, but neither did I need anyone's approval! I ***had to*** find my passion and dream!

In my studies, I was learning that various groups viewed God differently. Even among Christians—Baptists, Catholics, Methodists, Eastern Orthodox, Calvinists, Presbyterians, Armenians, Quakers, and Episcopalians—beliefs differed about Jesus Christ. Each denomination insisted their position was correct. But these were not the only viewpoints. Other religions like those practiced by the ancient Greeks and Egyptians, and modern day Hindus and Buddhists encouraged adherents to pray to their own masters the way that Christians worship Jesus. All had different perspectives, but one thing remained common: a universal belief in a Great Spirit, a Creator, regardless of the nature of the religion. It's a belief that there is more to us, a belief in our greatness.

Living the Dream

Sally came had been coming to see me about various issues, but all of our sessions were in some way connected to her religious beliefs. Every time we focused on the problem at hand, it traced back to her father's beliefs. He was a devout Christian who opposed her liberal spiritual beliefs, let alone her lesbian sexuality. Finally, after many months of dancing around it, I told her that she was going to release this issue once and for all. I knew she was ready to move on, but she needed a push! She had wonderful plans to use her massage therapy and energy healing skills and wanted to open a wellness center. I saw this wellness center in her! I knew it was time to make her dream happen. She was ripe!

In prior coaching sessions, Sally had understood that in order for the process to work, she had to come from an open, secure, confident space. She couldn't be wishy-washy about her healing center, especially when it came to attracting the right staff. She had to be in her power and exude the energy she wanted to bring into her center so her clients could connect with it and receive the appropriate healing.

"Sally, I want you to describe the vision you have for this wellness center," I gently coached her.

"It's going to be a place where everyone comes for the specific service they need to get the deepest healing. A place where they feel comfortable, they are at home, and they can just let go. We'll have services like acupuncture, Reiki, yoga, Tai Chi, massage therapy, life coaching, and meditation."

"And how will you be part of that center?" I asked her.

"I will be a practitioner, but more importantly, I want to be the example of healing. I want to show people that I did it, and so can they. I want to offer seminars to share my struggles, issues, experiences, and how far I've come so that they connect with the information in their own way and move past their struggles, too!" Sally exclaimed.

"That sounds great, Sally. And how will you help them when you come across a situation where they are living someone else's dream? Perhaps living their spouse's or parent's or sibling's vision for their life?" I asked.

"I will use all I know to show them the difference between what it would look like to continue along their current path versus what it might look like if they followed their heart and spirit. And I hope that by viewing the two scenarios, they'll be strong enough to follow their spirit," she explained.

"Ok great! Now tell me, Sally, what would it look like for you if you continued living your dad's dream and hiding your true self, versus living the life your heart and spirit desire for you?" I asked. "What would be the worst thing that could happen if you lived out your spiritual journey?"

The expression on Sally's face transformed from confusion to enlightenment. "Wow!" she said. "It totally makes sense now! I need to throw away the notion of living my dad's dream. I really need to follow my heart and spirit so I can live my own dream. Tina, I am finally ready to let go! I know that if I continue to try to make my dad happy, it will only be dishonoring my spirit's journey. I see it clearly now. Thanks!"

Are you ready to live your spiritual life? If yes, take the pledge. Write, sign, and post the following pledge in places you frequent such as your bathroom mirror, refrigerator door, meditation area, or car, etc. It's reminder from your spirit!

I pledge to cut the energetic cords with love and compassion from me to people, situations, and things that prevent me from living a spiritual life. By doing so, I allow others to find their way to living their spiritual life also. I pledge to LIVE MY SPIRITUAL LIFE.

Signed   Dated

Living Your Passion
... passion ... soul's purpose ...

Your passion is your indicator that your soul is on task, that it's doing what it came here to do. We all come to Earth to fulfill our soul's purpose. Are you fulfilling yours?

If your answer is "I don't know if I am," then you are not. Stop what you're doing for a moment and notice what makes you tick. As I am writing this book, I am filled with joy and excitement because I am doing exactly what I am suppose to do at this moment. I am not questioning whether this something I should be doing or whether I should be doing something else. I am immersed and having a great time taking the next step on my journey.

If you're questioning your purpose or the reason you are doing what you're doing, then it's time to make some changes. Try the following meditation and record your responses in your journal.

||||||||||||||||||||||||||||||||||||||||||||||||||||||||||||

EXERCISES
Follow your bliss.
— Joseph Campbell

Finding Your Soul's Purpose Meditation

Arrange a quiet environment without disturbances by turning off all technology, perhaps putting on soft music, lighting candle(s), infusing aromatherapy oils such as lavender which has a calming effect. Manage your surroundings so that you can relax, be still and reflect deeply. Have pen and paper handy for note taking afterwards. Get in a comfortable position, lying down or sitting up. Take long, slow and deep breaths—inhale and exhale. Focus on your breath for a few minutes focusing on your inhales and exhales. Every time you inhale, inhale positive, cleansing oxygen. And every time you exhale, let go of something with your breath. After a few minutes, you will achieve a rhythm of accepting positive inhales and letting go of emotions, patterns, beliefs, etc. that no longer serve you. Give yourself permission to go back in time knowing that this is safe and you are always in control of your meditation.

Go back to as early as you can remember as a young girl and boy. Try to recall the dreams you had for yourself. Don't force it. Just let the images and ideas come naturally. If you think you are imagining, that is just fine. Just go with it. Remembering to connect to your breath and ask yourself when ready:

What did my dreams look and feel like when I was so young? What did I imagine was possible in my future?

_____

_____

_____

What part of the dream do I still resonate with and how can I bring this back into my life now?

_____

_____

_____

_____

Which people in my life encourage me to follow *my* dreams? Why? How do my dreams overlap with theirs? How are they different?

_____

_____

_____

_____

What will it take for me to start living my own dream and stop being concerned about others' dreams for me?

_____

_____

_____

_____

What is the worst thing that could happen if I live out someone else's dream? What is the best thing that could happen?

_____

_____

_____

_____

What is the worst thing that can happen if I live out my own dream? What is the best thing that can happen?

_____

_____

_____

_____

Notes

Notes

Chapter 10

Where Are
You Going?

**Start by doing what's necessary; then do what's possible;
and suddenly you are doing the impossible.**
—St. Francis of Assisi

fter such a long time in my spiritual closet, I started
to assess where I was going, moving forward on my
spiritual path. I began to examine all my friendships,
social groups, and contacts, assessing which ones were carrying
me toward my divine purpose and which ones were hindering
me from reaching it. This was difficult, especially when it came
to my parents and siblings.

But I had to stop playing the hiding game: I had to be
my authentic self. So, I slowly changed my social calendar.
I started to spend more time with like-minded people. And
little by little, the others faded away. It was sad, in a way;
however, I knew that it was time to move on. Just like the
saying goes, "We meet people for a reason, a season, or a

lifetime." It was time for me to attend to my spiritual garden. I started by weeding out a lot of people from my life. I needed to plant friendships and relationships that would enhance my soul, and eliminate those that diminished it.

However, even though my friends changed, I still had to deal with the relatives, which was difficult, especially where my children were involved. I began to examine those relationships for my children's sake, not mine, but that didn't mean I had to suppress my beliefs.

I still had many lessons to learn, but I no longer had to agree with my family's beliefs; nor did I have to hide myself anymore. It wasn't like I took a microphone and made an announcement to them or that I threw my beliefs and truth in their faces. I just started living my life openly. I came out of the spiritual closet. And, of course, I began hearing questions, some of which were strong and provocative, with debate-like overtones. I simply answered them with my truth. And as soon as these individuals became aggressive or tried to get me to change my mind, I told them that I appreciated their opinions, and asked that they do the same and appreciate mine.

Sometimes this provoked furious attitudes. I simply stood tall and in my power, with love. I knew this was their fear coming through, and they were trying to learn how to deal with it. You see, not only were they teaching me to follow my truth, but conversely, I was providing them the opportunity to question whether their long-held beliefs were still their truth. The question of why they were so insecure when they claimed to have such great faith often crossed my mind. However, I knew that if I asked such a question, we would go off-tangent with the conversation.

So I often remained silent, knowing that eventually they would wake up in divine timing, just like I had woken up.

And who knew? Perhaps there were others among them who were still in the spiritual closet. I hoped that some day they would step out of their closets when they were ready as well.

Waking Up Spiritually in Our Own Time

My experience with my relatives brought home for me the futility of judgment or criticism. We need only love and awareness to understand that everyone will wake up spiritually in their own time.

Now here's the crazy part. As we become enlightened, we honor all races, creeds, and religions because enlightened people know that although we are all one, we all exist at different levels or vibrations. This does not make some of us superior or inferior; it simply means that we are all at different stages of awareness in our lives. Enlightened people know this, but religious people still seem to be trying to figure this out. They view their truth as the only way, which is a very close-minded perspective. As loving they may perceive themselves to be, they actually are ***not*** loving when they exclude the rest of us on the grounds that we believe differently from them.

If Jesus is love – and I truly believe he is! – and they follow Jesus, why do they not love all people, regardless of their beliefs? Why does religion limit, restrict, constrict, and ingrain fear, loving at certain times, but judging at other times? If Jesus forgave as many people as the Bible indicates, why would he all of sudden decide he was going to condemn some of us? What happened to "Do onto others as you would have done to yourself"? Are members of these religions really practicing what they preach?

Religion teaches us separation, that we are separate from God. There is God, and there is us. We're killing each other over these beliefs. We're killing each other in God's name! My intention here is not to judge others; rather, I am raising awareness by observing and stating what is happening around us.

How Do We Make a Difference?

And how do we handle people who oppose us? The answer is surprisingly simple: by being our authentic selves. By loving ourselves unconditionally and (learning to) love others unconditionally, in spite of where they are in their spiritual development. This is what a master or leader would do. We teach and enlighten by example. People's skills may just be lying dormant, but ready to awaken when they are shown by example. They may simply be asleep for a while. Perhaps they've even hit the spiritual snooze button a few times. My husband was like this before his spiritual awakening.

We never know when people will wake up. And if they awaken slowly, their spiritual progress and process maybe different than ours. Patience is a key ingredient in spiritual evolution. In the meantime, we need to follow our own hearts, passions, and spirits. We need to simply live our spiritual lives and honor our own soul's purpose.

Away from Jesus and Then Back Again

God and Jesus always played key roles in my life. I often heard from fellow Christian worshipers that there were no other figures. Jesus was King —and that was it! Jesus was the only one who saves. I thought to myself, "Really? *Our* faith is it?" I frequently thought about the millions of non-Christian people around the world. Where did they go wrong? Was it their fault that they were born and brought up in a non-Christian environment? What exactly were they up against if they didn't "believe?"

"Hell," many of my fellow Christians proclaimed. "They will not be saved; they will be damned." they added ominously.

What??!

I knew in my heart that had to be completely wrong. I believed in Jesus; however, I knew he was not the only aspect of God. There **had** to be more.

I occasionally challenged this limited belief system with various Christians whose answer was to keep referring me to the Bible. They also commented that I had better change my thoughts or I would be condemned, too. The more I heard this from people, the more I began to resent Jesus. I actually started turning against him. I removed the cross pendant I'd worn for years, and every time I heard someone speak Jesus' name, I would just walk away. I wanted nothing to do with him!

It's not that I didn't believe in Jesus – I just didn't want to hear it anymore!! "Who does Jesus think he his?" I often thought to myself. "How could all these people be brainwashed into his faith?!" I was so resentful of Jesus, his religion, and his followers.

That was when I began exploring other churches and religions. But attending many different places of worship didn't bring me any answers to my spiritual questions. So I took a break from running around and I started reading many different types of spiritual books, and I began to meditate. I dedicated blocks of time every day to this practice. I had small children, yet I made sure to carve out some time daily to follow my heart. I was beginning to understand that only I could answer my questions. Other people's answers were simply not doing it for me.

I also dedicated one full day, Sunday, to being quiet and shutting myself away from the outside world. While everyone else was attending their religious services and activities, my husband and I stayed home, turned off the phones, computers, and TV, and took time to go within. We started our isolation time at home. My husband was not quite as tenacious as I was; however, he also felt this was what we needed to do for ourselves. He was into the quest. So we dedicated this time as our "family day." We would read, pray, reflect, meditate, play with our kids, enjoy each other's company, rest and nap. Before long, we realized we had started something great! We began each week in a special way.

Our family was growing closer and closer with each "family day." Every week, we all looked forward to it. When our kids got older, we would hear them telling their friends that Sunday was family day and they would not be available. They started looking forward to our quiet, peaceful days together, and our home became our church on Sundays. Our family day became a spiritual service we provided for one another. Sundays are still our dedicated family time. With years of Sundays behind us, we have created a wonderful spiritual foundation, not only for ourselves but also for our kids to carry on.

Once we had established this foundation and began to feel reassured that it was really OK for us to create spirituality at home, I started to phase Jesus back into my life, along with other wonderful ascended masters. There is definitely room for all of them in my life. The guilt subsided and abated completely. How could anyone not see the beautiful spirituality we were creating in our family? Our family's spirituality was not only special, but also loving and caring, without guilt or fear. All the wonderful qualities Jesus possessed.

||||||||||||||||||||||||||||||||||||||||||||||||||||||

AFFIRMATION TO OWN:

Feel free to write, post and recite as often as needed. Having the intention of when you say it, you own it. The more you recite it, the more you live it.

I acknowledge that I am the creator of my spiritual happiness.

||||||||||||||||||||||||||||||||||||||||||||||||||||||

Standing Tall in Your Power

Hank, a husband and father of three, came to me for assistance. He had grown up in a very strict Catholic family. And his wife, Susan, was from a strict Jewish family. Neither felt that religion really did much for them, but both their parents were constantly telling them how they should live their lives. They felt their parents were completely disrespecting the way they chose to live, and they heard it from both sides all the time. They were tired of seeing their folks, or even answering the phone, since they knew the conversation was always the same: it was always about religion.

"How do I handle this?" Hank asked me.

"As long as you and Susan are congruent with your beliefs, you must take a stance not only individually, but also as a couple." I answered.

"We try. But they are always asking us all sorts of questions, and they claim they are specifically are afraid for our children's future. They're worried our kids won't go to heaven and all that," Hank explained.

"Are you and Susan concerned about your children's future?" I asked.

"Oh, not at all. We strongly feel that there is one God, and he loves all His people. There is really nothing to be afraid or guilty of," Hank answered.

"So why feed into some else's fear and guilt?" I asked.

"What do you mean?" Hank asked, perplexed.

"What I mean is that your parents are experiencing fear and guilt about what will happen if your kids do not follow in their footsteps. Explain to them that your beliefs and their beliefs are slightly different. You all believe in God, but you're all taking a different road to get to the same place. Also inform them that you're sorry this is bringing them so much discomfort and unhappiness right now. However, you and Susan feel strongly about your beliefs, just as they feel strongly about theirs. If they decide they want to learn more about your point of view, you will be happy to discuss it with them. Otherwise, you will no longer tolerate any judgmental questions or behaviors from any of them.

"Going forward, you will let them know that when they become judgmental and forceful with their beliefs, you will end the phone call or visit with them. Inform and assure them that you love them and honor their beliefs; all you're asking is that they do the same. Anytime they raise the conversation, you can ask them if it's a sharing/learning conversation or a judgmental one. The latter will cause the phone call or visit to end," I explained.

"Yes – that makes a lot of sense, Tina. But wouldn't that be disrespectful to our parents?" Hank asked.

"Didn't you mention to me that your problem is that they don't respect you and your beliefs?" I asked.

"Yes, I did say that."

"Well, respect starts with you. You inform and teach people how you want to be treated. If you want them to treat you with dignity and respect, then that's what you need to communicate to them."

One month later, Hank came in for a follow-up appointment. He had all sorts of stories to tell me about the parents. He admitted it had been difficult the first few times he'd had to take a stand and be in his power; however, he was noticing changes. Their parents kept trying to revert to the old patterns, but as soon as they did, Hank and Susan remind them of the deal, and their parents stepped up to cooperate.

II

EXERCISES

**If you keep going in the direction you are walking,
you will end up where you headed.**
—Zen proverb

Which path are you taking for your spirit?

_____

_____

_____

_____

If you don't know, when would be a good time to start figuring it out?

_____

_____

_____

_____

List some things you could change or enhance to create a more profound
spirituality.

_____

_____

_____

_____

Who might oppose your spiritual path or judge your spiritual views? Whom could you ask for more support on your spiritual journey?

_____

_____

_____

_____

Bonus: Download free exercises, meditations, tips, etc. at
*www.**TinaSacchi**.com*

||||||||||||||||||||||||||||||||||||||||||||||||||||||||

Notes

Chapter 11

Are You Ready to Come Out of the Spiritual Closet?

Wherever you are is the entry point.
—Kabir

*C*oming out is a time of awakening and accepting your spiritual destiny in a balanced way. It's about readiness. It's about being free, finally released from the restrictions, rules, and regulations that have constricted you. It is about loving and accepting yourself as an invaluable spirit. It's about honoring yourself, for when you honor yourself, you honor the world around you.

Determine what makes you happy on all levels, and take your best shot. If you question whether you need to come out then let me make it easier for you.

I, Tina Sacchi, give you permission to take the next step in coming out and connecting to your spirit.

Whether you come out of the spiritual closet all at once or take baby steps, your spirit is guiding you. It is your spirit that has nudged you to read this book and begin taking the necessary steps to finally be congruent with your soul's purpose.

Preparing Yourself

Coming out is a process of accepting your spiritual preference and first disclosing it to *yourself*. Only then, when the time is right, can you reveal it to your family and friends. This can be a confusing process, so take one step at a time. Questions about whether you will be discriminated against or ridiculed will probably cross your mind. This new lease on life will allow you to look within to assess what really makes you happy and which beliefs make you tick. This is an opportunity for you to evaluate who you are and where you want to be.

Inevitably, your circle of friends will change. Your family will very likely disagree with you. Some of them will try to convince you to change your mind. Some people may shake their heads in disgust, while others will simply think you're weird. Unfortunately, there will more than likely be those who voice their opinions about your decision with expressions like:

- You are a sinner!
- You will go to hell!
- You are going against Jesus!
- God will never forgive you! We will never forgive you!
- You are a disgrace to our family!
- We will disown you!
- We will leave you out of our will!
- You are an embarrassment!
- How could you do this to us?
- Why is God punishing me like this?
- If I knew you would do this, I would never have had children!

The list goes on and on …

Just remember that none of these remarks is yours to keep. They are all signs of other people's issues – not yours. Let the others deal with their stuff. No matter what they say, this is not about you; it's about them. Make sure you do not take ownership of their issues, or you will get stuck in the mucky vortex of negativity.

The truth is you will never be able to control how people react to you. All you can do is be honest about your beliefs and feelings. Jesus wants you to do this, for he speaks of love, not religion. So let love and your spirit be your guides. Think for yourself. How would Jesus behave toward these others? He would love them! So love them – and move on! But more importantly, love you first. If you cannot love yourself, it will be impossible to love others. So start with you!

Coming Out Timeline

Martin Luther King, Jr. has said, "Take the first step in faith. You don't have to see the whole staircase. Just take the first step." I think that's good advice. Be gentle with yourself. Don't put yourself on a deadline. There is no specific timeline or proper way to come out, other than doing it at a pace that makes you comfortable. Some of your friends and family will support your decision. Those who don't were never really congruent with your beliefs anyway. Many will eventually come around, but if they don't, this is the time to move on from those who won't or can't support you.

You may want to give your family members a chance to absorb the news. You've been brewing in the closet and it has taken you a while to come out, so you can't expect your loved ones to immediately support your decision. They may need time to catch up. Just be patient.

Before coming out, you'll want to determine whether you are going to make a complete break or slowly make your way out of your situation.

If you choose the complete break, then you'll want to plan for the worst-case scenario. In some cases, parents will throw their children (even adult children) out of the house! Chances are that things will not go as badly as all that, but as with any major life-defining event, it's important to plan ahead and play it out in your mind first.

Consider what you will do – where you will go if something like this happens. Can you afford your own place? If the answer is no, this is probably not a practical time to come out. Wait for now, but think about when would be a better opportunity to make this change. If you are a minor, your parents have jurisdiction over you. Ask them to seek professional counseling for the whole family.

Another approach is to slowly exit from your religious obligations. Starting by skipping weekly services and duties may be a more peaceful option, allowing your family and friends to slowly acclimate to your lifestyle. And if questioned about your religious beliefs, you can provide information on a need-to-know basis. You are slowly exiting without any major blows or confrontations. This way may make it easier for others to accept who you are.

A Spiritual Coming Out

My father-in-law had an urge to see us at Christmas 2001. They were living in New York and we were across the country in Arizona. This was right after 9/11 when terrorists crashed two airplanes into the World Trade Center in New York City. My in-laws lived about ten miles from the World Trade Center and felt tremendous shock and all kinds of emotions because it was so close to home. In fact, their emotions ran the gamut from confusion: "How can this happen?" To anger and revenge: "They will pay!" To insecurity: "Is it not safe to live in NY any longer?" To sadness, for all the lives that were affected and lost! Many people they knew experienced losses; it was a devastating and sad time, especially for them. Not many people were enthusiastic about flying immediately after 9/11. However my father-in-law sensed an urgency to see us for a few weeks.

One night toward the end of their stay, around 4 AM., my mother-in-law came to our room to wake us. "Pop is on the floor," she said. My husband and I bolted out of bed. My husband immediately began performing CPR while I witnessed this unusual energy surrounding Pop's body. I couldn't explain it then; however, now I know that it was time for him to cross over. There was an opening in our field for him to go. I noticed his spirit rising from his body, so I started arguing with him out loud. He was there in front of me and, I told him not to go yet, not to die in my house. "Go back to New York and die! Besides, it's your daughter's birthday. Do not die today. Die tomorrow!"

I was having this conversation while Joe was performing CPR, and my mother-in-law stood by watching it all. She finally jolted me out of my monologue and told me to call for help. Rescue personnel arrived immediately and whisked Pop to the hospital, where he was pronounced dead. What a shock! What a blessing!

You may be wondering: How could it be a blessing to have a loved one die – not to mention, in your house?! Let me explain.

We were all stunned and zombied out after the death. We started making phone calls back East, informing children, relatives, and friends of the sad news. I was in robot mode, making sure all the details were seen to, while my mother-in-law, still in shock, simply tried to make sense of it all. My husband was in his own zone, balancing and regrouping. Our kids, too young to really understand, were fine.

Joe decided to take a breather and went out to get pizza for us. About an hour later, he came home all lit up! Not alcohol-wise, but spiritually! He told us to hug him and feel his father. Without question, his mom and I went over to him and we gave each other a group hug. I felt an indescribable energy. Words can not accurately explain the presence we felt – it was so remarkable. It was inconceivable. It was electrifying, magnetic, warm, and loving, all at the same time. Joe was enlightened with his father's spirit.

He started to tell us about his encounter with his father. As he got into his car to pick up the pizza, his dad was sitting in the passenger seat. Next, the whole windshield lit up with Light energy. I had to stop myself for a moment. Perhaps you recall I mentioned that my husband had been on the fence about all this "woo-woo stuff." And now he was recounting this intensely spiritual experience.

Pop started to talk to him. First, he said that it was time for him to go. There was nothing anyone could have done to change that. Also that he was proud of Joe and his other kids. And he told Joe to make sure to tell his mother that he loved her. This was a bit much for Joe to handle, so he started flooring the car out of nervousness. Pop just told him to slow down! Joe was understandably a little shocked that his father was there, talking to him!

They arrived at the pizza place and Joe told his father to stay in the car, but of course Pop followed him into the store and continued to talk. So Joe kept telling his father to stop, but Pop was continuously talking to him. I could only imagine the employees thinking what a nutcase Joe was, since they must have thought he was talking to himself. They got the pizza and came home, Pop still communicating with Joe while he was driving.

After the group hug, Pop started channeling through Joe. When he entered Joe's body, Joe's mannerisms immediately transformed to his dad's! Using Joe's body and pushing Joe's spirit out, Pop spoke to his wife about things they had done together, stories about which only the two of them could have known the tiny details. It was amazing! He told his wife that she needed to continue on, that he would guide her and always be with her from the other side. Frankly, my mother-in law is a great individual, but she was not able to connect or understand what was happening. She thought her son Joey had lost his mind since his dad died, and this was how he was handling it.

I experienced mixed emotions. It was sad that Pop had left this physical world, especially from my house and on his daughter's birthday. I was still angry at him for that. But I was also feeling blessed that he chose my place to make his transition. I believe his spirit was ready to leave this physical plane; in spite of 9/11 and the difficulties flying, there was no stopping him from coming to say farewell and allowing us to experience his crossover and the messages he gave us from the other side. And he helped his son Joe experience something so deeply profound, no book or story could ever have conveyed it.

To witness my husband step off the fence and become turbo-boosted into enlightenment was one of the greatest gifts I have ever received. I was also envious that he'd experienced this so nonchalantly, while for years I had been studying spirituality in the closet! He had the blessing of becoming connected to Spirit through a single very important event.

I feel deep gratitude that Joe connected to his spirituality this way because it helped him better understand God and himself. It also gave me confidence, reassurance, and a husband who finally believed with his heart and soul in the same things I believed.

The biggest message I received through my guides and from my angels while Joe was channeling his dad over the course of almost three hours, was that I was here to enlighten those who wanted to be enlightened, but it was not my job to convince anyone. Wow, what a message! And what a relief! I had heard that before from my guides and angels, but the message was different that day. We were all touched by the Light. We witnessed a passing and a blessing. We had all crossed over to another level.

I connected to that message immediately. I was relieved from the burden of having to convince the world! I was here to enlighten only those who want to be enlightened. Really??! It's that simple? Yes and no. Yes, it was simple, because I resonated with this truth. This experience removed the burden, my blocked thinking that I was supposed to convince everyone and helped me realize that was not what I came to Earth to do. I knew I had a divine support team, and that my guides and angels would continue to nudge me along my spiritual journey. And it wasn't simple since I knew that a lot of changes and shifts were going to result in myself, my family, my friends, and my social environment. And changes did happen …

I began meditating a lot and inquiring within, connecting with my spirit and my guides and angels even more. I took more classes and started to meet people who were interested in having me doing energy healings. I was still slowly emerging from my closet.

Giving up the burden of needing to convince everyone relieved me and opened up my path further. I realized there were so many people who needed direction, and that was where I should put my energy. My spiritual journey was to assist those people who want my guidance. In recognizing that, I was moving forward spiritually.

Following Your Spiritual Path

When Mary came to see me, she was experiencing depression and anxiety, so much so that she felt she was no longer able to function. It took her hours to get ready for work, and she was always late. Any time off she had, she spent in bed, just trying to get through the day. She shamelessly admitted she had thoughts of not wanting to live anymore. She had been to psychiatrists and had been on medications for a couple of years.

"What kind of work do you do?" I asked.

"I'm a school counselor at a Christian high school. I've been there for about three years," she said.

"How do you like being a counselor?" I asked her.

"It has its ups and downs," she explained.

"Tell me all about the ups."

"Well, the ups include that I am interacting with people, which I love to do. I am an integral part of their lives. When I can make a difference in a child's life, it's so rewarding!"

"So, what are the downs?" I asked.

"Some of the kids do not want to be there, and talking with them is like pulling teeth. I can't help anyone who doesn't want to be there," she said. "It's so frustrating! Plus, in our district, we are not allowed to use some techniques I know would work and that the students might actually enjoy," she explained further.

"What kinds of techniques?"

"I would love to use hypnosis, meditation, energy healing such as Reiki, various crystals, that kind of thing," Mary said, describing her ideas.

"Wow, that sounds beautiful and very healing," I said. "So what would it take for you to use the techniques you mentioned?"

"Oh, I could never use those techniques there! It would be frowned upon by the school."

"So why do you continue to work there? Do you realize there are other options?" I asked.

"Well, I get full benefits there, good money, and I follow the school schedule with time off," she explained.

"I see what you're saying, Mary. However, you haven't really enjoyed the extra time you get, have you? You've been going in late and having a difficult time enjoying the time off you do have. So I'm not really seeing any benefit for you of having this time off in that environment.

"Can you imagine yourself in another job, utilizing the skills and talents your spirit has given you to use? Your spirit is using your body as a signaling tool. It's getting your attention by letting you know that you've gone off track with your purpose. Is it possible that your spirit would be happiest if it were implementing the techniques you mentioned you would love to use?"

"You're right! I haven't taken any advantage of my time off. I've really just been trying to survive the days. But what about the money I'm earning? I am paid very well," she said.

"How have you been spending the money?" I asked.

Suddenly she realized, "A lot of it has been going to medical bills."

"How much goes to these bills?"

"About $150 a week," she responded, surprised.

The finance expert in me suddenly emerged. "So, what, you're spending $600 a month, or $7,200 a year on medical bills? Do you realize that you actually earn more than $9,000 to net $7,200 in after-taxes income to pay for these bills? That means you could maintain the same lifestyle making $9,000 less a year. Can you imagine yourself somewhere else, perhaps earning less money, but being happy, loving your job, and being free of depression or anxiety?" I asked.

"The way you put that makes so much sense. You've made it clear for me. But how do I make the change?"

"We take it one step at a time," I told her. "The first is acknowledging the possibility that there is another way. The succeeding step is to emerge from your box and explore the possibilities. I can help you, if you'd like."

"Yes, please!"

In just a few life-coaching sessions, we were able to get Mary to a place of happiness and satisfaction. She now works at a metaphysical college that is open to all of her techniques and ideas. She is also taking advantage of the opportunity to learn new skills, a benefit of being employed there. Occasionally, Mary comes in for a maintenance appointment, and I feel elated that she has made so much progress in such a short time. With approval from her doctor, she is off medication. She wakes up early and heads to work with a smile. She's back on track, moving forward and following her spiritual journey!

||||||||||||||||||||||||||||||||||||||||||||||||||||||||||||

EXERCISES

There is only one moment in time when it is essential to awaken: that moment is now.
—Buddha

Create a meditation time for yourself without interruptions where you can be alone and quiet.

Optional: In a dimly lit room, surround yourself with candles, aromatherapy, soft music, incense, pillows, blankets, anything you need to make the space as comfortable as possible.

Sit or lie down. Keep a pen and this book nearby. If you are alone, it will help to record your meditation and play it back, while you close your eyes, relax, and let go of all other thoughts. If you have a spiritual buddy who is emerging with you or if you are in a group, you can take turns helping each other.

If this is a group activity, your partner can guide you through the following intention simply by reading the instructions as you settle into your deep, quiet space. As he or she guides the meditation at an appropriate pace, he or she will interject the questions below so that your subconscious mind can use them to clear anything that may be in the way.

After the meditation is over and you come back from your deep state and are reconnected with your physical body, you can complete the questions below in your journal. I would encourage group discussion or sharing with your partner to see others' perspectives and learn new ideas that might assist you.

MEDITATION
Use the following as a meditation to help you find your spiritual focus.

This is a time for relaxation that you dedicate just for you... a conscious effort to relax as completely as possible.

As you get into a comfortable position, you gently close your eyes. Focus on your breathing. Imagine noticing your lungs expanding as you inhale, and with every exhale, notice your lungs release and relax. However you imagine your lungs is perfect. However you imagine yourself inhaling and exhaling is just perfect. Allow yourself to breathe in cleansing, calming oxygen and letting go with every exhale. Inhale and exhale deeper and slower each time. Refrain from worrying about any of the things that are happening in your day-to-day life as this is a time for you to let go and relax every muscle, fiber, cell of your being. For this meditation time that you honor and dedicate to yourself, you allow yourself to completely relax and let go. You are always in control and safe and now you choose to relax deeper and deeper with every breath. And as you relax deeper and deeper, you can let go of anything that doesn't serve you any longer so that you can live better in the present.

If you mind wanders off, take note without judgment and bring it back to your breath. Inhaling. Exhaling. Aware of your lungs miraculous breath performance. Knowing that miracles are happening to you all the time. Knowing that trust and faith can create more miracles in your life. And as you breathe in and out, you say to yourself the following:

I am on a spiritual path, moving forward with my heart. My head will tell me, from time to time, to analyze everything, but my heart always knows best. My heart is connected with my spirit. So if my heart always knows, then my spirit knows as well. There will be people I meet along the way who do not understand. That is OK. I am not here to convince them. I am here to enlighten myself and those who want to work and walk with me on this spiritual path. I am here to love myself unconditionally because when I do, I am honoring my spirit and my Creator. And when I love myself unconditionally, how can I not love others the same way?

When I love myself and accept my faults and correct them, I can learn from them and move on. I can do the same for others. When it comes to my final day on earth, I want to leave nothing undone. I want to leave with a satisfied soul, a soul that came to earth and completed its tasks and purpose. This way my soul evolves and I can be more and more creative. I am headed toward positive energy, love, peace, harmony, joy, fun, laughter, and humor; my spirit loves this. My spirit needs to experience these things in order to evolve. And not only for my evolution, but for others' as well. If I am happy, all the people around me are happy, too. The energy is contagious.

I'm ready to deflect negativity in any form – whether mental, emotional, physical, or spiritual. I am here to bring peace and love to the One. We are all connected, so if I bring peace and love to myself, then I also do that for others. Not only to humans, but also to animals, plants—all living things. I am here living a spiritual life, holding space for others' growth and mine, as well. I am here not to judge anything or anyone. I am here to love and be loved, to honor and be honored. I am. I am.

And now you take some deep, slow breaths bringing awareness to your physical body. Wiggle your fingers and toes. Know that you have the power to hold onto things that don't serve you any longer, and you also have the power to let them go. With gratitude and appreciation for all the lessons you learned in the past, you gently let go, creating space for the new opportunities and possibilities. I am. I am.

In your journal, record any revelations, findings, ideas and inspirations,
Assess your positive and negative emotions. Write down all the emotions that you imagine feeling when you come out. Compare the two and see what it will take to bridge both worlds.

Emotions I Am Feeling Now	Emotions I Imagine I Will Feel	How To Bridge Both Worlds
Restricted	Free	Seek like minded people/group

Bonus: Download free exercises, meditations, tips, etc. at
*www.**TinaSacchi**.com*

Notes

Chapter 12:

Many Masters and Leaders

**If you knew who walks beside you on the path
you have chosen, fear would be impossible.**
— A Course in Miracles

There have been many masters and spiritual leaders, from Jesus and Buddha and Krishna to Mother Theresa, Gandhi, and Martin Luther King, Jr. These wonderful beings have served and dedicated their lives to spirituality; they've devoted their time and energy to creating peace and love among us. Unfortunately, many among us have argued over who is authentic and who is not. In fact, what we've been doing in response is rather barbaric. We've been chopping people's heads off in the name of God.

If we were to turn things around and put our energy into enhancing, rather than degrading, we would have a better planet to call home. I often wonder what aliens must think when they observe our primitive actions. They must shake their heads in disbelief, saying, "In divine timing, we hope the Earthlings will get it."

This is not a case of who is wrong and who is right. Who cares?! This is a time for making the changes that our past spiritual leaders worked so diligently to begin. Let's pick up where they left off. Let's move forward instead of continuing to look backward.

The truth of the matter is, whether we're white, black, yellow, or green, we all want to experience love. We all want to live love. We all want to smell love. And when love is jeopardized, we feel threatened, insecure, uncertain, and fearful. Then our primal fight-or-flight instincts get activated, and we fight. Since this has been going on for hundreds of thousands of years, this is what man knows and this is what man does: fight.

If we were to look into each individual's eyes to see whether or not they are an enemy, we would see instead their spirit— their spirit that is part of God. We are all connected! So by killing them, we are killing ourselves. There is no "us" and "them." There is only us. We are all one!

If we hate them, we hate ourselves. If we judge them, we're judging ourselves. When we honor them, we honor ourselves. And when we love them, we're loving ourselves. It really is this simple. Too simple, in fact. It takes human beings to make it complicated. Let's start simplifying things. We are all one!

Jesus speaks of love, not religion – so let love be your guide. Think for yourself. What would Jesus do to others? He would love his enemies!

Ask Jesus to help you see others' spirits, not their personalities. Our power comes when we work from the heart.

Buddha and Krishna

When I started coming out of the closet, I read about many masters and leaders. Whether they had ever taken physical form did not matter to me.

One master who really resonated with me was Siddhartha Gautama, the founder of Buddhism. Later called Buddha which means "one who is awake," he was a spiritual teacher born around 563 BC on the Indian subcontinent. Some people call him the Enlightened One. Based on his own experience, the Buddha saw that all human beings had the capacity to purify their minds and to develop infinite love, compassion, and perfect understanding. He shifted attention from the heavens to the heart and encouraged us to find solutions to our problems through self-understanding. This was exactly what I wanted to do! This was how I wanted to live my life! So I read more on Buddha, bringing all of his teachings that resonated with me into my soul.

I also resonated with other beautiful beings such as Krishna, a deity worshiped across many Hindu traditions from a variety of perspectives. As with all of God's prophets, Krishna's message is the one of love. In fact, none have ever taught that war and hate are good. Every one of them agrees that love and acts of loving kindness are all that matter. This is what I believe too!

I also believed in angels, messengers from God who help us when called upon. Daily, my list was growing longer and longer as I invoked their help. Simultaneously, I was getting more resolute in my determination to live and speak my truth. It didn't matter if some of my masters were of different religions. What mattered to me was that their energy was good and that my heart and soul resonated with them. Their light made me stronger and wiser and helped me live my truth. My spiritual reality insisted that I come from a position of integrity.

Precious Earrings

My close friend Trudy was born and raised in the Jewish faith. We grew up together in Brooklyn. Trudy and I celebrated all of our holidays together. When it was time for the Christian holidays, such as St. Anthony's Day, Easter, and Christmas, Trudy would join my family and me in our festivities. When the Jewish holidays came around, I would celebrate Passover and Rosh Hashanah with her and her family. She attended mass with me, and I went with her to services at her synagogue.

At Passover, we would keep Trudy's front door open and set a place at the table for the prophet Elijah to come and visit, as is traditional during a Seder. This I found fascinating and so spiritual. I tried to sit next to Elijah's chair at the table, in hopes of feeling his presence. I was open to new experiences, and Trudy's family was open to having a gentile at their table. Likewise, when Trudy came to my family's religious functions, we were open to having her join us in ceremony.

One day, Trudy called me up, frantic. "Tina! I lost my great-grandmother's earrings at work. I've been all over this building, inside and out, and I can't find them. I've taken every elevator that leads to my office, and still no earrings. I've even checked the lost and found, and they're not there. My mother will kill me if she finds out, especially since she told me not to wear them. I need your help with St. Anthony, Tina. I remember that you found your lost bracelet a few years ago by praying to him. How do I ask him for help?"

In Catholicism, St. Anthony is the patron saint of lost objects. Catholics honor him with great respect and celebrate June 13, St. Anthony's Day, with feasts around the world in his honor. I have enlisted his help many times, and Trudy was well aware of the respect I had for this special being, even though he died in the thirteenth century.

"Trudy," I said calmly, "take a breath and relax. You need to create an intention, knowing that by praying to St. Anthony, you will find those earrings. Can you do that?"

"Yes, I'll try," she said.

"No! You can't just try. You need to **believe** this is so, that St. Anthony can help you and that you will find your great-grandmother's earrings. Can you do that?" I asked.

Trudy started laughing hysterically. "Why are you laughing?" I demanded.

"Because I am Jewish, and I believe in St. Anthony. It's just so funny," she said.

We both laughed at how ridiculous this would probably seem to other people. However, Trudy and I saw each other as equals, without the separation Jewish and Catholic religions can foster among their members. We honored each other's spirits. And so we prayed to St. Anthony, asking him for guidance in retrieving these special earrings. And in return, Trudy promised that she would contribute to the St. Anthony group I belonged to so that others could be helped financially.

A couple of days later, Trudy decided to try her building's lost and found one more time, and there were the earrings. My Jewish girlfriend was happy, and her belief in an ascended master, St. Anthony, was deepened.

||||||||||||||||||||||||||||||||||||||||||||||||||||||||

EXERCISES

**Many masters chose to come into a physical body
to inform us about the Christ consciousness
Our biggest teachers ... religion and its followers
God is love and omnipresent. God is everywhere
and in all people, places and things.**

—Author unknown

With which masters and leaders of our time (e.g., Buddha, Jesus, Krishna, Mother Teresa) do you resonate, and why?

_____

_____

_____

_____

_____

Which specific qualities or aspects of the masters and leaders cause you to resonate with them?

_____

_____

_____

_____

How can you begin incorporating these qualities or aspects into your own life and spiritual practice?

_____

_____

_____

_____

How can you see your life enhanced spiritually by incorporating ascended masters into your practice?

_____

_____

_____

_____

Bonus: Download free exercises, meditations, tips, etc. at
*www.**TinaSacchi**.com*

||||||||||||||||||||||||||||||||||||||||||||||||||||||||||||

Notes

Part Three

Tools for Moving Forward on Your Spiritual Journey and Eliminating Religious Guilt

Chapter 13
Spiritual Tools

"Prayer is one of the greatest and most excellent means of nourishing the new nature, and of causing the soul to flourish and prosper."
—Jonathan Edwards

*J*ust as a plumber, carpenter, or electrician carries essential tools when making house calls, a spiritual person like yourself can create a spiritual tool box to help you along the road to spiritual self-discovery. It's easy. Find a box, basket, or bag and add notes, articles, and techniques you come across that you can refer to when you need direction and clarity. Since having spiritual tools at your possession is essential for moving forward on your journey and eliminating religious guilt, I have listed in this chapter some of those that I've found most effective for my students, clients, and myself. Try each one out to see what works best for you. You might find that several help you move in the direction that you yearn for.

Prayer

I learned about prayer at a very young age. My parents always prayed at meals and in the evening. We prayed at church, school, and home. The neighborhood women would congregate outside our house since we were centrally located on the block, and sit on our stoop with their rosary beads where they all prayed together. We also lit candles everywhere—in church, at our house, and at others' houses. And we prayed some more.

We always came together and prayed. I have memories of everyone praying during the Vietnam War when an older cousin was drafted. My grandfather even built an altar out of balsa wood, and we would pray there too. Prayer was part of our lives. And it still is. I may not pray the same way I did in the Catholic years. But I do need to give credit for my Catholic education which instilled prayer in my life.

You can pray alone or in a group. One way is not better than the other. Solitary prayer has its benefits. It's a wonderful time to gain perspective on your individual situation, create reflection time, and connect with God in your own unique way. Sometimes we all need alone time. But when you come together as a group of as few as two people, prayer can also be very powerful. As a group you may pray more and/or learn other ways to connect. You combine your collective energies and the presence of this energy can be felt at the deepest level of your being. It's like sharing a special meal with like-minded people. We come together to share our thoughts and feelings. Like breaking bread together, communal prayer feeds our spirit.

Prayer attracts solutions. Why? When you simply dedicate a time to pray, you focus on the situation at hand. And when you focus, you are dedicating all of your self—that is your mind, body, spirit and emotions. By focusing and praying, you can relieve stress, calm fears, and reduce anxiety. You gain clarity as a result. You open yourself to possibilities, insight, and inspiration. Praying on a regular basis helps your overall health and well-being.

Invoking or Calling Upon God

One of the first things I do upon awakening in the morning, meditating, before meals, before meeting with clients, before any workshop/class that I am teaching is to call upon God and my Divine support team. I know that there is more than just me to make it all happen. My faith in God is real and powerful. I believe that each day I am learning in this human physical body, and that God and His helpers are on my side. I know I have freewill to call upon them or not, and so I do with all my heart. It's better to have more beings rooting, nudging, and comforting me than just me being there all by myself. This is true for you as well.

Open Sacred Space

One way I invoke spirit is to open my sacred space. This means I am calling upon all of God's helpers from all the directions: south, west, north and east, earth and sky. With them, I create a bubble of protection, and comfort—a sacred space dedicated just for me—so I can proceed through my activity with their love and guidance.

When you open sacred space, you focus on the present moment, putting all your "to do" lists away, leaving the busy world outside, and connecting with your spirit and your Divine helpers. There are many ways and rituals to do this. You can even open sacred space with a simple one second thought. But there is something special about performing an action. It sets the mood for what's to come. You are also taking the time to show respect and honor. I like to compare it to taking a bath.

You can take one at anytime by turning on the faucet, filling the tub, and cleaning yourself with soap and water. However your mood is enhanced and the experience is more helpful when you light candles, diffuse aromatherapy, use soothing oils, dim the lights, and play soft music while in the bath. Both activities accomplish the physical task of cleaning your body. However on a mental, emotional, or even spiritual level, the second way can be more effective. The pampering and nurturing reduces stress and promotes well-being.

It's the same with opening sacred space. Whether it's a one second thought or a specific routine, as long as you do it with heartfelt intention, the space is sacredly opened. A few of the many ways I open sacred space follow. Feel free to create your own way or adapt my suggestions below to suit your own needs. It's all about invoking with intention and heart energy.

Invoke One of the Three Following Openings With Intention:

I.

I invoke the light of the God within me
I am a clear and perfect channel
God is my guide.
God and I are one.
Thank you.

II.

Clear Me. Shield me. I invite the Holy Spirit, guides and angels to be present. Thank you.

III.
A Prayer for Opening Sacred Space Individually or with a Group

This is a shamanic ritual used by Native Americans and others—medicine people, energy healers—throughout the world. Though it is longer than the first two intentions, it will help you create the time to get into the process. This prayer can work for you individually or it is a possible way of initiating a group into sacred space.

I face in each direction, starting with the south, with heart energy, sometimes using a rattle or a drum for a few seconds. Then I sip and hold water in my mouth and blow it out using my breath. Another way is to put the scented water in a spray bottle and spray it in the direction I am facing. Scented water can be purchase or you can create your own by adding oils such as sage oil to water. Or, I smudge sage. This is the process of burning dried sage and fanning the smoke with a feather or other object in the designated direction with sacred intention to purify the area. Finally, I call or say a prayer of invocation to God, our guides, ascended masters, and angels to come and join me. At the end of each prayer, I say "ho," "amen," "and so it is," or "Namaste." I then move onto the next direction until I've completed the four cardinal directions, the earth and up to the sky. Here is an example:

South

To God and the helpers of the South, including Archangel Michael. Please come and show us how we can shed our past that doesn't serve us any longer. Show us how we can walk with heart. To the helpers of the South, please blow through us in this space now. Ho.

West

To God and the helpers of the West including Archangel Gabrielle. Please come and protect our medicine space. Show us how to walk with impeccability. Teach us to be without judgment, neither judging ourselves nor others. To the helpers of the West, please blow through us in this space now. Ho.

North

To God and the helpers of the North, Archangel Uriel, Grandmothers and Grandfathers, and Ancient Ones. Show us how to drink directly from the nectar of life. It is our birthright. We honor all of you, those that have come before us and those that are yet to come, even our children's children. To the helpers of the North, please blow through us in this space now. Ho.

East

To God and the helpers of the East and Archangel Raphael. Come to us from the place of the rising sun. Show us the mountains we only dare to dream of. Teach us of our spiritual destiny and how to fly wing to wing with the Great Spirit. To the helpers of the East, please blow through us in this space now. Ho.

Earth (Kneel or bow down to the earth)

Dear mother earth. We're gathered here for healing. And we know that every time we heal ourselves we heal the world around us. And we honor all our relations, the Stone People, the Plant People, the two-legged, the four-legged, the winged, the finned, the furred and the clawed and even the creepy crawlers. Thank you mother for always holding us on your belly. Ho

Sky

Father Sun, Grandmother Moon, Star Nations, Star Brothers and Star Sisters. Put your love, your light and energy upon this circle. Great Spirit, you who are known by a thousand names, you truly are the unnamable One. Thank you for bringing us together to sing the song of life. Ho

When you have finished this invocation, release all the helpers by closing the sacred space in each direction. Follow the same procedure as for the opening, thanking them all with heart energy.

In any of the preceding or following tools, the assumption is made that you have called upon God each time and therefore have opened your sacred space.

Accessing and Resolving Your Subconscious Mind

If you learned how to ride a bicycle at the age of 5 and you didn't ride again until you were 15, do you think you would know how to do it? Of course you would! The program or record of how to ride a bicycle is stored in your database or your subconscious mind. Your physical body is different at 15 years old. Every cell and muscle is different, but the memory or record is intact and it has an energy or emotion attached to it.

In fact, it's helpful to think of your subconscious as your database: All of your records are stored there—records from this morning, yesterday, last week, last month, last year, decades ago. Indeed, your subconscious holds your skills, all your life experiences, memories, patterns, behaviors, imprints, and impressions. These records have certain energies or emotions attached to them. Some of the records are of happy times and so good and loving energies are attached to them. Some records are not so good and so an energy of sadness, disappointment or even anger may be attached. Changing the energy or emotions of the records stored in your subconscious leads to changing your outlook and feelings. You will always have the memories. However, you will replace the emotions or charge behind an unpleasant memory with something much more positive.

This positive change is totally up to you. Your mind is very powerful, and it can create whatever you desire. If you believe this, you can reprogram your subconscious so you may be able to live life at its fullest and achieve anything you desire now—even a spiritual life without religious guilt!

Let me use a more mundane example from my family's life. I have pleasant memories of riding bicycles. When I first learned, I struggled just for a bit to find my balance. However, once I got it, I loved the freedom and speed I derived from learning this new skill. My son's experience was totally different. He struggled with balancing the bike and crashed into a parked car. To me it looked as if he had lightly bumped the car, but to him this was major crash that traumatized him. As a result, he wanted nothing to do with bikes for years. His experience (record) of bike riding had different emotions associated with it than mine did. To him, it was an unpleasant activity—the opposite of my experience.

Years later, after intently watching his friends ride their bikes, he consciously decided to overcome the fear. He took a different approach—a slow one, that included many observations of others riding their bikes without crashing. He proceeded with caution and was able to achieve balance. Finally, he experienced the freedom and mobility bike riding brings. His outlook changed by deprogramming his first stressful experience and replacing it with a pleasant one. He did it!

Observing Your Subconscious Mind

Your conscious mind is responsible for logic and reasoning. It controls all of your voluntary actions. So if I ask you to add some numbers like 1 + 6.5 +3, your conscious mind will give me an answer of 10.5. And if I ask you to take four breaths at a fast pace and four at a very slow pace, your conscious mind will take control. However if you don't put your conscious mind on your breathing and you just breathe naturally, your subconscious mind will take over. No logic or reasoning needed.

You can activate and observe your subconscious by allowing your conscious mind to get bored and restless. If there is nothing to compute or analyze, your conscious mind becomes passive. You know this to be true from experience. Consider how many times you've asked yourself whether you shampooed your hair in the shower. Or how many times have you wondered, "Did I put detergent in the washer?" Or, "How did I get from my house to the office without remembering the drive?" These oft repeated behaviors allow your subconscious mind to come alive. At first when you learned how to drive, your conscious mind needed to be involved. You had to make sure you were seated in the right position, the mirrors were perfectly adjusted, the key went into the ignition and turned to a certain point, and the transmission was placed in drive. Now after hundreds or thousands of driving experiences in your subconscious mind, you accomplish these steps without consciously thinking of them. As soon as you enter the car, the activities are automatic.

Another way of understanding how the subconscious mind works occurs when you change the location of certain things in your home—say the utensils in the kitchen or the furniture in the den. The first few times you have to consciously remember where you put them. So for instance, you need to navigate around the recliner now when you didn't have to before. And if you put your kitchen utensils in a different drawer, you will have a repeated conscious awareness of where they are before the new location gets impressed into your subconscious mind. And once it's there, no further conscious thinking is involved. You simply go to the new drawer and pull out the soup ladle.

Reprogramming Your Subconscious Mind

With the power of intention and using consistent repetition, the subconscious mind will eventually accept what you **want** to impress upon it. The key words are intention and want. It's all about free will. For instance, if you are going through a spiritual transformation, it may help you to read about how others survived their own religious and spiritual issues. You might take classes or attend events that lift up your spirit. It's helpful to surround yourself with like-minded people. There are many ways to reprogram your subconscious mind. The following are some of my favorite tools.

Repetitive Observations

My son kept observing his friends riding their bikes successfully for five years! As he watched them, he filled his subconscious mind with positive reinforcement. He noticed that they had fun and that none of them "crashed" nor did they fall off their bikes. He realized that he could do the same. Yes, it took him that long to figure it out and be comfortable with it. But it's important that he worked it out in the end. He did it his way, at a pace that was comfortable for him. You will have your own pace in your spiritual development. Go with your own flow to achieve positive results.

Affirmations

Positive affirmations are positive sentences you repeat many times in order to impress your subconscious mind and trigger it into action. Your every thought and word are affirmations. So when you state an affirmation, you consciously take part in it. The repetition then becomes embedded in your subconscious mind and forms a record. Whatever you think or say creates more of the same. So be careful what you wish for. Choose your words and thoughts consciously so that your subconscious mind will act accordingly and you get what you really desire.

In addition to spirituality, there are many broad areas in which affirmations may be used such as self-esteem, love and relationships, creative self expression, work/vocation, prosperity, health, and spiritual development. Establish in your mind the specific area in which you most want to improve or which goal you most desire attaining. By working with affirmations, you commence the process of changing negative and unproductive beliefs into positive life supporting beliefs that with regular practice will create a desired future.

Affirmations must be positive! Observe how different

- I hate this house.

is from:

- I am grateful for this house since it gives me shelter and security.
- I am open to a new house now which resonates with my spirit.

Keep your affirmations in the present tense. If they are set in the future with statements such as "I will be" or "I will have," your desire or wish will always be waiting to happen.

How effective is this affirmation?

- I am going to live the spiritual life I desire some day.

What about this affirmation?

- I am living the spiritual life that is innate in my being.

Clearly, the second affirmation is better. Maybe you're wondering, how can I say something that isn't true now? Well if you keep anchoring the truth in the future, it will stay there—something you want to do "someday." However if you state what you desire in the present tense, you will start owning it today.

My favorite affirmations begin with "I am." These two little words place a tremendous power upon your affirmations. You are intentionally directing the affirmation to yourself by saying "I" and whatever you state after "am" is what you own. All day long you can add whatever you want to "I am":

- I am healthy.
- I am loved.
- I am beautiful inside and out.
- I am honored and respected by everyone.
- I am deserving of happiness.
- I am spiritual.
- I am living in a world of my own choosing.

In order to ensure the effectiveness of your affirmations, repeat them with attention, intention and outcome belief. If you say to yourself that you are *going to try using affirmations however you doubt they will work,* you are only affirming the negative, and this will not help you reach your most cherished desires.

Several years ago, a woman in her 60s cleaned my house for a few months in exchange for some life coaching sessions. Lori was between jobs and needed help. She claimed that her previous employers treated her poorly and put her down all the time. Almost all of them had laid her off. She wanted to solve self-esteem issues and feelings of unworthiness.

One day I went about my business in my home office while Lori went about her housekeeping duties in the next room. Occasionally I would hear her talk out loud and say things such as: "Lori, you're so stupid." "I am an idiot. I can't do anything right." "You will never amount to anything."

I would cringe every time I heard these defaming words. It astounded me to know that this woman would consciously say these things to and about herself. And the more she said them, the more I knew her subconscious mind was confirming these words through her daily life.

After a while, I stopped what I was doing and invited Lori to sit down with me. I repeated each negative statement she'd made about herself. "Lori," I asked, "why are saying these things?"

"Because I was born that way," she replied.

"How were you born?"

"Without Jesus in my life. I have no right to be religious."

This startled me. "How so?" I asked.

"My mother got pregnant when she was 14 years old," she continued "and my father left. I never met him. I was looked upon as a bastard."

Years ago, it was greatly frowned upon to be born out of wedlock. Society, especially among certain religions, viewed this person as an outcast.

"I was raised by my grandparents. They always said since I was a bastard, I had no right to anything. Not even going to church. They were ashamed of me."

"What about your mom?" I gently probed. "Did she say these things too?'

"My mother was young, and we all lived with my grandparents. She went along with what they did and said."

I knew I had my work cut out for me. I had to show Lori that she was just like anyone else born into this world regardless of whether her parents were married. She had all the rights to believe in any religion, she had a right to be spiritual. No one was going to condemn her, but she was condemning herself.

Using all the subconscious tools at my disposal such as positive affirmations, hypnotherapy, meditation, I helped Lori achieve balance, peace, and acceptance of herself. She realized that her grandparents were repeating similar pattern of their ancestors and really didn't have the capacity to think outside the boundaries that were handed down to them through generations. They actually did do the best they could in coping with a situation that was out of the ordinary for them.

As Lori changed the way she thought about herself, she made great progress in her life. Eventually, she was hired as an administrative assistant at local company, and she's still working there. She also found a non-denominational church which welcomed her with open arms. She has gained much confidence belonging to this world and especially to God. She occasionally comes in for maintenance sessions, and I admire all the work she has done to get to this new self-actualized state. And her words now are nothing but positive. When she walks into my office, she greets me with: "Tina, I am the best and I am living a terrific life."

"You are the best and you deserve it," I always reply.

Meditation

How many times have you felt that your body is here, your mind is there, and your emotions are somewhere else? This is true for most of us. In fact, I often start my spirituality classes with a grounding or connecting meditation. When the participants arrive, they are physically in the room with me. However I feel that their minds and emotions are still at home where they just left their children. Or maybe they're still at work noodling on a problem. And so I conduct a meditation to help the participants get connected again.

We've all heard of the mind-body-spirit connection. The purpose of meditation is to connect your mind-body-spirit and your emotional body too. It also sets the tone of the day. Most people awaken and start their day going from 0 to 60 mph! As soon as their alarm clock goes off, they either hit the snooze button several times (which tells me that they are lacking sleep) or they bolt out of bed. Do you start your day at that frenetic pace? If so, then most likely you have set the tone and you will race through the rest of your day, not only physically but emotionally, mentally, and spiritually. If you walk out of your house in the morning without brushing your teeth, that would be yucky. Well, it's the same with meditation. If you don't meditate or set the tone first thing, you will most likely have a disconnected or yucky day.

I love to start my day with a meditation—even if it's only for a few minutes. As I become aware that I am waking up or as my alarm clock's soft music awakens me gently, I know not to open my eyes but to lie in bed and connect to a place of gratitude, peace and love for myself and for all those people I will come in contact with throughout my day. I like to take advantage of the stillness in my body as I awaken by setting the tone and intention for my day. I need to be in this deep state for meditation. So rather than awakening myself totally and then trying to get back into a meditative state, I lay in my bed for an extra five or ten minutes.

Most of the time, you'll probably need just a few minutes especially if you make this your daily routine. Set your alarm 5 to 10 minutes earlier than normal so you don't rush through it. This is the time for you to set your daily tone and intention. If you need more time at first, treat yourself to it.

Meditation is also helpful for you to obtain answers and clarity—not from the outside world—but from within yourself. All of your answers are there. Who knows you the best in the whole world? No one other than yourself! If you keep running around and all the days of the week streak by at the same pace, how can you get any clarity? How can you find answers when you're moving so quick?

There are physical benefits to meditating as well. The practice normalizes blood pressure and reduces your heart's work load. It reduces stress, lowers cholesterol, improves air flow to your lungs, decreases muscle tension, increases serotonin production which influences mood and behavior, and enhances the immune system.

All you have to do is intend for your body to relax and it will respond automatically. It doesn't take long. Close your eyes, take a few deep and slow breaths, and allow yourself to release the stress or tension in your body. Talk to your body and give it permission to relax. You can start from anywhere. My favorite spot is my toes. I say, "My toes are relaxing, my feet are relaxing, my ankles now relax, my shins relax," and so on, moving up the body until I've instructed every part to relax. You can repeat this anytime and will achieve peaceful benefits.

You are in control of your body. If you want to wiggle your toes and fingers at this precise moment, you can do so. They move because you are in control. The same goes with instructing your body to inhale relaxing, healing oxygen and let go of stress with every exhale. Repeating affirmations as you breathe, such as "I am relaxed, peaceful, and calm" or "I am spiritually supported on my journey by the Universe" is a great combo!

As you meditate more and more, eventually you will find that you can meditate anywhere. Sprinkle your day with moments of connection. At work, find a few minutes to connect. Even in the bathroom! Go for it. I can meditate virtually anywhere, even at busy airports. At home, create a sacred place for yourself to meditate. Even though I have a healing studio where I see my clients and students, I often go to the corner of my bedroom which I have designated as my place to meditate and reflect. I've meditated there thousands of times so now, as soon as I sit on my pillows, I immediately go deep. I have created a conditioned response or a learned pattern. In fact, even when I'm not home, I sometimes think of my meditation corner, tune into the feelings of relaxation, and I instantly go within.

Evening meditations are also ideal. It helps me sleep better without disturbances since I set the intention and tone to have a restful, relaxed, deep, and pleasant sleep. You can sit or lie in your bed or meditate in another spot in your home.

The more you meditate, the more you will find your life has inner peace—a peace you've created. And when you live with inner peace, if life become challenging, you can make decisions from a more poised and calm place. Difficult situations will become easier to deal with. You will naturally and peacefully make the right spiritual decisions for yourself regardless of other people's opinions. And when you have inner peace, you experience it through a feeling of happiness that is innate in your being. I call this spiritual bliss.

Steps to Take
- Minimize or eliminate distractions
- Choose a quiet place to meditate
- Create a peaceful, environment. This is your place so you want to tailor it to your liking:
    - Play soft, soothing music if that will help you
    - Light candles if you'd like

- ◆ Use aromatherapy essential oils such as lavender oil which has a calming effect.
- Keep a journal/writing pad and pen nearby.
- Lay or sit in a comfortable position. If you're sitting in a chair, keep your back straight with your feet flat on the floor if you can. If you're sitting on a meditation cushion, you can crisscross your legs, again with your back straight.
- Set the intention: If you need an answer to a question or situation, write the question with the intention of obtaining an answer in this meditation. If the meditation is meant to obtain more inner peace, then set that intention.
- Some people like their eyes partially closed and others like them totally closed. Experiment and go with what makes you comfortable.
- Some people like to focus on a lit candle. Whatever works for you is perfect.
- Pay attention to your breathing. Breathe naturally, slowly, and deeply, preferably through the nostrils, without attempting to control your breath. Become aware of the sensation of the breath as it enters and leaves the nostrils. Allow yourself to take breaths and with every exhale, let you body sink right down. I say to "allow" and "let" because you are the one who is doing this. No one can allow or let this happen but you!
- Soften your face and body. With each breath, worries and concerns fade away.

At first, your mind will be very busy. You might even feel that the meditation is making it busier; but in reality you are just becoming more aware of how active it really is.

Imagine there is a basket in front of you. Place all the things that are taking up your attention into the basket. Place all the things from today, days and years gone by, worries for the future. By putting all these thoughts in the basket, you can open yourself to clarity and opportunities for insight and inspiration. If the basket gets full, then allow yourself to create a larger one or more baskets. You'll find as you do this, that you will become lighter and lighter. There will be a great temptation to follow the different thoughts as they arise, however focus on your breath and keep filling your basket. If your mind wanders off, take note without judgment and immediately return it to your breath. Repeat this as many times as necessary until your mind settles on the breath. Remember to breathe and float down and sink down so that you get to a deep place of peace and connection.

Sometimes all you need to do is write in your journal or writing pad what is taking up your attention so that you can become freer. Your journal can act like the basket. Just keep writing things down as they come across your mind so that you can free your mind even more. You will find that by dumping them out on paper, you will eventually get it all out, and you will get to a point of quiet and stillness.

You can also chant (see below) or recite a mantra (repetition of a sacred word/phrase). This helps you place you focus on the words or the sound. A popular mantra is "om." You can say it slowly annunciating and expanding the sounds.

You can do all of the above or take one or two of my suggestions, experimenting as you meditate so that you find the right combination, each time remembering that what works for you today, may be different tomorrow.

When you get to the place of stillness and quiet, stay there for as long as you can. At some point, ask yourself the questions you wanted answers to. Notice what happens when you pose the question in your mind. Notice the people who pop up. Jot these down briefly and close your eyes again. Keep retrieving information from within as you focus on the question or intention.

Guided imagery is another type of meditation. This requires no effort except following words from the audio that you are listening to. Some people start their meditation practice this way. It's a great way to get you into a relaxed state using images recited by another person. Just remember, the more you meditate, the more secure, confident and peaceful you will become.

My client Wendy came in one day after working on so many different things, like anger, resentment, abandonment.

"So Wendy, how's going?" I asked

"All the anger, resentment and abandonment issues I had in the past are gone. Thanks so much for helping me release all that," she said.

"What is coming up for you now?" I asked

"My job is stressing me out, and I feel uptight. I want to be calmer and more relaxed, spiritually, connected, and adaptable. I miss going to church, but I don't have time or energy to go."

"Adaptable? What do you mean?"

"Well there are a lot of changes at work. Our job descriptions keep evolving daily, and I find it difficult to adapt and accept change. I am tired of it," Wendy explained.

"Are you physically or mentally tired?"

"Both. No matter what time I get home, I am exhausted and irritable each evening. And I wake up tired as well."

I asked Wendy about her sleep ritual.

"What do you mean by ritual?" she asked.

"Your routine. What do you do for yourself before you fall asleep?"

"I eat and watch TV in bed. Most often, I fall asleep while watching TV, I guess around midnight. There is a part of me that feels like I need the TV to fall asleep."

"What do you usually watch on TV as you're falling asleep?"

"Mystery and crime shows that I record each day. I love them!"

"And what time do you get up in the morning?"

"My alarm goes off 6 AM, but I don't get up until 6:20. And then I am rushing out of bed. I get dressed and go to work. I put my makeup on either in my car or at my desk."

"What about breakfast?"

"I either wait until lunch or I buy something at the vending machine."

"When do you meditate?"

"I haven't lately," she admitted. "I know I need to. I feel better when I do."

"Do you know many hours of sleep you *need* each night?"

Sheepishly, she answered, "Eight hours."

"Well let's look at the picture that you are creating, shall we? You are telling me that you need 8 hours of sleep and you get 6. That means you are sleep deprived each night by 2 hours. You keep hitting the snooze since you are tired, however that makes it worse because you are not getting restful sleep. Furthermore, you set the tone of your sleep by watching mystery and crime shows and so your dream state is not resting but working through the night.

"Now I am going to describe to you a possible sleeping ritual. You need to prepare to sleep," I explained. "First of all, the only things you do in your bedroom are prepare to sleep, sleep and have sex. That is it! At 10 PM, you turn off all TVs, technology, etc. You are allowed to play music. However choose music that is soothing, relaxing and meditative. You can light incense, and/or diffuse relaxing aromatherapy such as scented oil. Put on your pajamas, dim the lights, wash, and brush your teeth as you listen to the music and smell the relaxing oils. Get out the clothes that you are going to wear the next morning. Massage lotions on your body as you sit or lay on your bed. Repeat affirmations such as: 'I am calm, relaxed, spiritually connected and adaptable throughout my nights and days.' The affirmation will become a mantra and/or meditation for you. You are setting the tone for yourself. How does this sound?" I asked

"Very relaxing. Can I add anything to this?" Wendy asked

"You can tweak this to whatever you want. It's your sleeping ritual."

"I want to put a hot towel over my face while I listen to music and smell the oil."

"Perfect! That is a great idea. I think I'll add that to my sleeping ritual too! And let's add another item. When you awaken in the morning, take a few minutes to set the tone of your day. Meditate for a few minutes."

I did more subconscious work with hypnotherapy so that Wendy could give herself permission to let go of the old unhealthy sleep patterns. We reinforced the fact that she could fall asleep on her own, independent of the TV or anything else.

Wendy came in a month later for a follow up. "I feel so rested," she said. "My sleeping routine is engraved so deeply into my schedule that I want no one interfering with it. I even took the TV out of my bedroom and created space for a table that contains all my sleeping ritual items: aromatherapy oils, lotions, music player, incense sticks and burner." In addition, she had been attending church more and felt the spiritual connection.

Mantra Chanting

Chanting is not a religious activity, although it has been used by Christianity, Hinduism, Buddhism, Judaism, Islam and other religions. Chanting means reciting or singing words or your deity's name repeatedly. It's a great way to meditate. Just a couple of minutes of chanting daily can completely eliminate stress, anxiety and tension. But before chanting a mantra, create an intention that is heartfelt. Some possible intentions can be:

- To connect or unite With God
- To honor God
- To meditate on a Deity or an aspect of the Divine
- To attain clarity on a certain situation
- To gain calmness by reducing or eliminating stress and anxiety
- To quiet your mind
- To invoke peace or protection
- To reduce negative energy or to dispel negative emotions such as sadness, resentment, anger, etc.

There are so many things you can chant:

- OM – A sacred sound which represents God, the source of all existence.
- Om Mani Padme Hum – a popular mantra that has many meanings. To me it means "May all beings enjoy the spirit of enlightenment."
- Repetition of prayers for the holy rosary is the Christian version of a mantra. An example is: Glory be to the Father, and to the Son, and to the Holy Spirit. As it was in the beginning, is now, and ever shall be, world without end. Amen.

How to chant?

With your eyes preferably closed, sit silently in the cross-legged position or take any comfortable position. (See the meditation section above for more details on creating an environment conducive to relaxing.)

Start chanting a word such as "OM" or a deity's name such as Jesus, Krishna, or Yahweh. You can even chant your own name. Take your time in saying the word and place emphasis on all syllables especially prolonging the last syllable.

Place your entire attention on your breathing. Be conscious of each breath that is exhaled and inhaled.

Chant until you feel complete.

When I chant, I often play a mantra audio and I recite along with the singer. I do this many times while I am getting ready in the morning in my bathroom, as I take my shower, and get dressed. Try this. You will notice that along with your heartfelt intention, it sets a wonderful tone for the rest of your day.

Retreating

Retreating means going solo for a few hours, a day, or longer. Retreats, especially in nature, facilitate deeper levels of introspection and awareness when you add moments of stillness. They create a time for renewal away from the hustle and bustle of life, away from technology, TVs, computers, cell phones, smart phones, iPods, iPads, you name it.

Retreats are a time and place for renewal. I encourage you to create the space in your life for taking full advantage of the opportunity to connect to yourself. This can mean going technology-free for one day. With all the technology available to us today, there are many ways for people to contact us— emails, texting, cell phones, faxes. Don't get me wrong; I love technology. It does save time, trees, and fuel. But this technology occupies us all the time. I witness many people constantly texting and talking on their cell phones even in the company of others. How can you truly tap into your breath and your spirit, and live a spiritual life if you don't take the time to literally smell the roses? If we are too busy taking pictures of the roses or texting someone else about these gifts from spirit, a spiritual disconnection happens.

It's important to take quiet time for yourself so that you can go within, retreat and be. There needs to be a balance. When was the last time you turned off everything?

Self-Hypnosis

A hypnotic state is a very relaxed state that can be even as deep as sleep. Remember, your subconscious mind is active 24/7 and therefore always aware of its environment and surrounding information. You use self-hypnosis all the time. Recall how you forget your commute from home to office? You are in a hypnotic state! Your analytical or conscious mind is passive. That is what we are trying to achieve with hypnosis.

Hypnosis or hypnotherapy is a state of mind in which you are highly responsive to suggestions or direction. This can result in the modification of your behavior and the thoughts occurring in your subconscious mind. You become extraordinarily suggestible in your subconscious mind when you are ready to make changes. Therefore you are always in control and you must want and allow changes to happen. My new hypnosis clients are sometimes afraid that they are going to cluck like chickens or bark like dogs with hypnosis. I've never seen this happen in my office yet! If you don't want change, then it won't happen.

Self-hypnosis is a combination of many tools affecting the subconscious mind that I shared above such as intention, affirmations, meditation, etc. There are many ways to perform it. The following is one way that many of my clients love to use:

1. Create a quiet time so you will be undisturbed. Similar to meditating, you can surround yourself with soft music, aromatherapy oils, crystals, etc. Always have a pen and pad handy so you can record any inspirations or revelations. Decide if you are going to lie down or sit in a comfortable position.

2. Decide on one objective that you want to accomplish before you begin. If you have many issues, then you can address them in other sessions. As described in the affirmations tool section, remember to make your objective positive and in the present tense such as, *"I am here to release the issue of feeling guilty in letting go of my family's religion."*

3. Create an affirmation using present tense and positive words: *"I live in a world of my own choosing. I choose my own spiritual way."*

4. Create the end result statement. Describe how you want to feel after the session is over again using positive words and the present tense. *"I feel relieved from past thoughts and memories that have held me back. I feel free and peaceful."*

5. Now relax your body by beginning to take slow breaths. Inhale and exhale.

6. Use a suggestion such as: *"I am relaxed and comfortable and with each breath that I take I relax deeper and deeper. My whole body relaxes from head to toe."* (You can name each part of your body and consciously breathe relaxation into it, i.e. my eyes relax, my ears relax, etc.)

7. Once you feel relaxed, combine your affirmation with your suggestion and the end result statement using the

intention that your breath will relax you even deeper. So it can go like this:

Breathing in and out slowly: *"My neck is relaxed. I live in a world of my own choosing. I choose my own spiritual way… I feel relieved from the past thoughts and memories that have held me back. I feel free and peaceful."*

Breathing in and out slowly: *"My shoulders are relaxed. I live in a world of my own choosing. I choose my own spiritual way… I feel relieved from the past thoughts and memories that have held me back. I feel free and peaceful."*

Breathing in and out slowly. *"My chest is relaxed. I live in a world of my own choosing. I choose my own spiritual way… I feel relieved from the past thoughts and memories that have held me back. I feel free and peaceful."*

Breathing in and out slowly: "My stomach is relaxed. I live in a world of my own choosing. I choose my own spiritual way…. I feel relieved from the past thoughts and memories that have held me back. I feel free and peaceful."

Essentially you are not only modifying your behaviors and thoughts at the mental level, you are making changes at the physical level as well. You are reprogramming each physical part of your body with the suggestion, affirmation, and end result statement.

Self-hypnosis is a powerful spiritual tool. A session can last for 15 minutes or more. Stop when you feel complete and satisfied with your session. If you question whether you are done, you are not. Continue for a few more minutes. Enjoy this state for as long as you want. When you're finished, record your experience by writing or drawing it out. You will get more mileage from your session since you've created the space and environment for your subconscious to be in releasing or healing mode and journaling will take it further.

Energy Healing and Clearing...Go Within

The field of energy medicine or energy work is extensive and expansive. In fact, different types of energy healing and clearings have existed around the world since the beginning of time. More and more energy healing techniques are developed as we evolve because all individuals have different energy makeup which is uniquely expressed in their own way and interpretation. It doesn't matter whether energy healing has been derived from traditional or scientific facts, since all techniques are based on the premise that everything is made up of energy. If everything is made up of energy, then we are energy. So if you give attention to that energy by focusing on it, you can change or shift it positively or negatively.

Another premise is that energy attracts energy. If you are a negative person—you are putting out negative actions, thoughts or energy—you will attract negative people in your life. If you are a positive person, then positive people will automatically want to be with you. Yes, there are times that negative people want to dump their stuff on positive people. This is how the term "energy vampires" came to be. However, most positive people will not allow that. Instead they gently nudge negative people in a positive direction without getting energy sucked out of them,

Energy becomes depleted in many ways such as confrontations with loved ones, unpleasant experiences, memories, behaviors, patterns caused by unhappy life events and situations. In theses cases, you need to clear the incongruent energies and replenish yourself with positive and healing, loving energy. An energy clearing and healing session with a healer can restore you.

One of my favorite energy healing and clearing techniques that became a catalyst for my spiritual development is the ancient technique called Reiki. Reiki (pronounced ray key) is a complementary healing that can be used in conjunction with any other medical or alternative healing technique. You can do it on yourself or someone else can perform a Reiki healing on you. It is administered by laying on hands (touch therapy), connecting with a person's energy points or chakras. The act of laying hands on the human or animal body to comfort and relieve pain is as old as instinct. Human touch conveys healing. However the touch doesn't even have to be a physical. It can be an energetic touch by hovering your hands or intention near the person's energy body or aura. Reiki allows everyone to tap into an unlimited supply of life force energy to improve health, enhance the quality of life, for stress reduction and relaxation. It's a way to work with your Divine Source. It's an enlightening teamwork experience that creates balance and relaxation.

You never know when or where you can use Reiki. Years ago when my younger son and I were shopping, he had an emotional outburst—a tantrum—in the shopping cart because I wouldn't buy him the sugary cereal he wanted. He had been a super colicky baby, and he'd had incidents like this since infancy.

A tantrum can be typical behavior for a three-year-old, but it was not something I wanted to experience in the supermarket. And so there I was, laying my hands on him for about 10 minutes, channeling the Reiki energy healing in the middle of the grocery store with people scurrying all around me. The healing was not only beneficial for him; it was also good for me. It gave me time (as a busy mom) to relax and get centered and balanced. When you channel energy, it's a win-win situation. The healer and the receiver derive many benefits. After the ten minutes, my son turned up his little eyes to me and said, "Thanks mommy, I'm all better now." I felt a renewed energy within me as a result. I kissed him and finished shopping. Later on that day, I did more Reiki and he continued to be relaxed and fine.

Find a professional Reiki Master like myself with whom to study so that you can progress to doing your own Reiki healings and clearings. My children and husband practice Reiki on themselves. Anytime one of my sons gets upset or distraught, his brother directs him to do Reiki on himself. This adds another benefit: while practicing Reiki on oneself, a person goes within and reflects. So instead of my children seeking guidance from others, they can achieve balance and obtain answers on their own.

One of my goals is to spread this beautiful healing technique to anyone interested so that they can use this tool at anytime and any place and heal themselves. To date, I have taught thousands of people and they are all over the world, spreading Reiki to others. I feel honored and humbled in the deepest part of my spirit since I am fulfilling one of my spiritual purposes here on earth: to enlighten those who want to be enlightened with a gift that they already have.

There are many energy clearing techniques available. I hope I have whetted your appetite. Follow your heart and spirit as to which one is best for you.

||||||||||||||||||||||||||||||||||||||||||||||||||||

EXERCISES
My biggest fear was that I would come to the end of my lifeand discover I had lived someone else's dream.
—Karen Blixen

Below is a list of spiritual tools discussed in this chapter. Feel free to add others. Prioritize these tools in order of preference and incorporate them in your life now. Use a journal or the "notes" pages at end of this chapter, to record your experiences. The more these activities become part of your routine, the more you will connect to your spirit and your spirituality.

Spiritual Tool:	Priority	Start date	Notes:
Prayer			
Open Sacred Space			
Affirmations			
Meditation			
Mantra Chanting			
Retreating			
Self-Hypnosis			
Energy Healing			
Other: Laughing			
Other: Play/listen to Music			
Other:			
Other:			

Bonus: Download free exercises, meditations, tips, etc. at
www.TinaSacchi.com

Notes

Find Your Authentic Spiritual Self

**God made so many different kinds of people.
Why would he allow only one way to serve him?**
—Martin Buber

The trip I took to Florida as a teenager that I described earlier in the book had a profound impact on me—I learned that a whole world existed outside my neighborhood's narrow view of life which was often governed by strict rules and rituals. As I grew older and continued to travel, I realized that I was doing exactly what the spiritual master teachers of all times—Jesus, Moses, St Francis of Assisi, Buddha Mikao Usui—did. Why were they always going somewhere? They had left their homes to seek out how they could be more spiritual, more connected, and bring the message back to others. I realized that when we get out of ourselves, our comfort zone, our routine, our rituals and rules, we begin our true spiritual journey. We go out in order to embrace our greatness. We find out who we are, our authentic spiritual self. We can discover our own spirituality and what it means to us, not just what it means to our parents, guardians, and ancestors.

Is It Religiosity or Is It True Spirituality?

One of my family members – let's call her Peggy – attended Mass every Sunday and sometimes a few times a week, depending on which religious holiday it might be. She wanted everyone, including her spouse and children, to spin their lives around her Sunday Mass schedule.

Peggy never missed a Sunday service. "To do so would be a sin!" she would announce to anyone who would listen. Even when she was on vacation, she went out of her way to find a church so she could dutifully attend services.

I began to notice, though, that when Peggy was outside her church environment, her actions were incongruous with her much-professed religious beliefs. For one thing, she didn't speak to some of her in-laws because of things they had "done" to her. In fact, she believed her in-laws were completely wrong about everything. She also despised certain family members and friends because they, too, had done her wrong. She did have some tolerance for her own family, though.

I witnessed these behaviors over the course of many years. And yet this woman was supposedly Christian. As in, Christ-like. But wait. Didn't Christ love everyone? I often wanted to ask her what she thought about when she attended church. Did her beliefs change once she left the church building? Or maybe she knew someone who'd given her permission to act in such a non-Christian way?

Peggy was a role model, according to my family's elders. She was the holy one. She was the religious one. "Really?" I thought. How is she getting away with all of this? If she can carry so much judgment and ill will and still be considered holy, it must be so much easier for me!

I, who don't want to attend her church, but live a spiritual life and give everyone the benefit of the doubt because I believe people are always doing the best they can, can grow deeper in my spirituality. I just don't want to attend services in the church building she visits or listen to people discuss one particular way of thinking. I want to choose my own spiritual guides and discuss **my** way of thinking. I can do that anywhere – I don't need to go to a specific building. I also really understood, perhaps for the first time, that my spiritually was different. I have a different perspective than Peggy and her co-believers. I see people as spirit first, not with their faults up front. I see beauty, even if it's hidden under a person's trials, tribulations, and life events. I am able to use my heart to forgive and move on. In Peggy's church, I wouldn't be able to that.

I realized that I could do much more than just attend a brick-and-mortar building. I could start my spirituality within, and then spread it to others by my words and actions.

I thank God for Peggy, because she showed me the difference. She showed me what I didn't want to be while simultaneously nudging me in the direction I did want to go. You see, sometimes your biggest teachers are the ones who boldly show you the dark from the light. And yes, the ones who irritate you the most.

Ways to Unwind Negative Emotions and Beliefs

Before you can find your authentic spiritual self, you will need to unwind old beliefs. Unwinding means to undo or being undone after winding or being wound. It also means to undergo a transformation or a change of position or action. So in order to unwind yourself of old beliefs, you must have been wound with them in the first place.

In my practice, I work with energy. Energy comes in different forms such as patterns, beliefs, imprints, impressions, and behaviors. If a person has a pattern of anger, I can't say, "Well let me cut the anger with my scissors and take it out of you so you can be free and live a more peaceful life." Anger is intangible. You can't physically bottle or remove it. Instead, it's a feeling, an energy. It shows up when you bring to mind certain thoughts, experiences, and situations. A specific thought will trigger anger each time you recall the circumstance. And every time you do, your subconscious mind is accessing the record of the thought and informs you that you always act out in anger when that record is retrieved. So you keep winding it tighter and tighter with more anger each time. Unless, of course, you consciously decide to unwind it.

I remember when a family member whom I will call Aunt Samantha would question me each week about whether I attended church. She would call me every Sunday evening asking, "How was mass today?" She did this knowing that I no longer attended church regularly.

I remember my insides heating up yet trying to remain calm so that I wouldn't raise my voice and be disrespectful to her as she was my senior. I also had a feeling that other family members had egged her on. Each Sunday, when the phone rang, I would both cringe and boil inside knowing that she was probably on the other end. And each Sunday, I would wind more anger and resentment into my being. The phone would just have to ring once, and I was fuming regardless of whether she was on the line. I was wound so tightly that eventually my husband would make comments like, "Oh that's right. It's Sunday evening. That's why your attitude." After he mentioned this several times, I knew my anger was affecting my husband and kids. I knew that I had to do something about it.

To have spiritual freedom, you need to release old beliefs that bind you. It's best to start with the awareness that each time you think of a person or situation, you have a specific emotion such as anger. Then consciously decide that it's time to let go of that emotion since it's preventing you from having the life that you want to live. You will use some of the tools I have already described and some that I explain below to get you through it.

Know that you are unwinding at your own pace. Some issues take longer than others. You are peeling away layers of the onion one at a time, to connect to your authentic spiritual self. If you are resisting layers and can't let go of them, use the tools I provide repeatedly, perhaps with a supportive friend or friends. Maybe you need to learn and understand all angles of the issue at hand. Perhaps there is a deeper lesson for you. Learn it and move on to spiritual freedom. Be patient, and I promise that as you unwind, you will gain clarity, calmness and peace within. Some of the following techniques may help.

Write a Dear John or Jane Letter to Your Religion from A Place of Heart

Hopefully you do not stay in relationships that no longer serve you. Religion is also a relationship, so why would you remain in a religion that doesn't meet your current needs? Write this letter as if you were breaking up with a lover. Be sure to include how you've benefited from having this religion in your life, even if it means you had hardships that taught you how to experience certain emotions. Without this religion, you wouldn't have gotten all this experience. Pour out all your feelings on paper. Don't hold anything back. Express all the details good and sad. This may take a few sittings. Simply start the letter, put it down, and resume at another time. You will know you are done when you are done. And then, you can burn the letter, rip it up, shred or bury it so it will be mulched into the earth. The important thing is to release anger, resentment, bitterness, ill will or any other negative emotions you have within.

Write a Letter to Your Parent or Influential Person Trying to Hold You Back or Hold You in the Religion

This may also take several letters. However you are still unwinding yourself to your authentic spiritual self. It's important to address each person that you care about. Again, like in the religion letter, describe this person's great talents, love, and inspiration. End with: "What I really want is your love, support, and approval so we can live harmoniously together without judgment." Note that this activity is for your self-healing and emotional expression and not for actually giving these letters to the people holding you back.

Use a Mirror

They say eyes are the windows into your spirit. Your spirit is the navigator of your life. By looking into your spirit, you are staring at the truth head on. Consequently, I often use a mirror with my clients to help them explore who they really are. By talking to themselves in the mirror, their feelings reflect back to them. I can determine resistance instantly because it is difficult for them to say or reveal certain things out loud. By looking in the mirror, they are also connecting with their spirit.

When was the last time you looked in the mirror for one minute not for the purpose of putting on makeup, brushing your teeth or doing your hair but with the intent to connect with your spirit? It's not surprising how many people have not looked in a mirror for more than a few seconds. And when I tell my clients to look at it for a minimum of 10 minutes, they usually start squirming after only 30 seconds. That's because they're not used to connecting to their spirit, their truth. As time goes on, it becomes easier and more comfortable for them to talk to their spirit. And their truth will set them free.

Mirror Exercise: You will find that this exercise can be done repeatedly. Each time you do it, you will go more deeply into your spirit.

Get into a comfortable position, making sure that you will not be disturbed. Have a note pad, pen, and tissues nearby. Yes tissues. They are there so you can let out your feelings, if you choose, with tears. Take some inhales and exhales, giving yourself permission to dedicate this time just for yourself and to explore what your spirit wants you to know about your spirituality. You can even prepare questions in advance.

As you intently look into your eyes and converse with your soul, you will connect and notice feelings and thoughts that may come into your awareness. Do not automatically dismiss them. Address each one as it pops in. Take notes whenever you need to. You can even set a timer if you find it difficult to be in front of a mirror for a long time. Try 2 minutes for each question, feeling, or thought you are addressing. If you need more time, then take it. The purpose of the timer is to get you to stay on task longer.

Some questions you can address with your spirit:

- What does my spirit want?
- How do I feel about religion?
- How do I feel about spirituality?
- What are commonalities between my old religion and my spiritual self?
- What are the differences between my old religion and my spiritual self?

- What do I want that I do not have spiritually?
- What are the rules in my home surrounding religion and spirituality?

Use Your Journal...Write it or Pour it Out...

Typically we try to problem solve through the conscious mind, the analytical process. But it's also effective to explore the creative and imaginary perspective, namely the subconscious mind. Journaling or writing affords you the opportunity for unexpected solutions to seemingly unsolvable problems. It helps you to understand another's point of view and you just may come up with a sensible resolution to the conflict.

It doesn't matter whether you write in an official "journal." You can use a word processing program on the computer, paper, pen, or even crayons to explore thoughts and feelings around religion and spirituality. Go as deeply as you feel comfortable. It's important to get out what you can to explore, learn, and dump any obstacles or baggage. This will clarify your thoughts and feelings. In fact, journaling will help you fully explore, release, resolve, and heal the emotions involved and engages both your conscious and subconscious mind.

Don't be a perfectionist or be concerned about penmanship, readability, the type of paper used, or grammar and spelling. That is not the goal here. Rather, you are looking for self-knowledge and the ability to let go of anything that is not in your best interest and highest good. And when you're done, you can burn your writing, bury it, rip it up, or delete the computer file. You are creating space so that you can be open to new opportunities and possibilities.

If you'd like you can give your journal a name since through your writing you'll discover that your journal is a friend that will always be available, ready to listen. How about Penelope or William? They are ready to listen.

Imagine the Perfect Spiritual Life

Your imagination is a healing tool that resides in your subconscious mind where all your skills, your life experiences, memories, patterns, behaviors, imprints, and impressions are stored. Young children use their imaginations all the time. Some invent imaginary friends to help them cope with certain situations, keep them company, and play with. As they do this, they are constantly deprogramming their subconscious mind on their own. They innately experience healing. Imagination is essential for our mental body since creativity would be impossible without it. Imagine not having any books, movies or TV shows that someone created using imagination? How would it be? What would life look like? How would it feel?

You see, you just used your imagination to change your perception momentarily. A possible imagined scenario might go like this: Well if there are no books, movies, or shows, then TVs, DVDs, movies, and games would not exist. News and stories would reach us in a different format. If there are no shows or movies to watch, we would spend our time in other ways. Or life would be pretty dull. Your imagination can go even deeper, since feelings will be created with each thought you choose.

Now use your imagination in a different way. Take some deep breaths to help you relax. When using your imagination to manifest and create a reality in your life, it's best to imagine with all your senses: sight, hearing, smell, taste, and touch—and even your sixth sense, your spiritual sense, your instinct or intuition. Your sixth sense is your gut feeling. I call it an internal spiritual signal that guides us.

Imagine what living the perfect spiritual life would be like using all your senses with specifics. It's important to fill in all the details of the people in your life, your environment, and activities. Record your imaginary findings in your journal and the exercise section below. Remember to have the faith and trust in your Divine Support team and release your prayers knowing they will be answered in Divine Timing, in its perfect time and space.

Informing Your Future Self
Using Your Intention and Imagination

How do you see yourself in the future?

Write a letter for a future time (one week, one month, 3 months) to your future self. Seal the letter, self-address and add postage and give it to a trusted friend. Note a date for your friend to mail it to you. Or if you prefer, seal the letter and schedule a time on your calendar to open it. When the letter arrives, carve out some time for you to meditate, journal and reflect. During this quiet time and without judgment, take account of how you've changed since the date of the letter and what changes you would like to make from this moment forward. Then begin the process again: write another letter to your future self. Each time you will notice progression.

In each letter include a beautiful greeting and salutation. Write messages of hope, peace, love, and encouragement. Include affirmations; state your goals so you will be reminded at that time and anything else you feel your future self would need to read. Add how courageous and lovable you are to make this monumental change! Share your hopes and dreams.

Write the letter just as you would write one to your best friend about how it feels to be you today describing in detail the present moment without predicting the future. Note that your physical body changes, and so does your mind. Each letter will contain its own wisdom. Things that are so important to you today, your future self may view as trivial. This is fine since it indicates how much progress you have made. When you have made a collection of letters, you can dedicate another reflection time to read through them chronologically. This will help you appreciate your changes and growth.

<u>Focus on the present moment—today not the future as much. Your letter can include answers to the following questions:</u>

- What are your religious vs. spirituality views today?
- What are your fears surrounding letting go of religion?
- Who is your support system, i.e. people, groups, etc.?
- What are the unanswered questions currently in your mind?
- What feelings predominate in these times?
- How do you feel about your spirituality and the world around you?
- What do you enjoy about today?
- What are you thankful for?
- What spiritual goals have you set?
- How do you expect to change?
- How do you expect to be the same?
- What are the lessons learned and advice for yourself?
- What advice would you give to your future spiritual self?
- What revelations have you had lately?
- What important lesson did you learn recently and don't want to forget?
- Have you come a long way?
- How connected are you to your spirituality?

—Sample Letter—

Dear Future Me of April 2012,

How have things been? I hope you're in a better spiritual place.

Do you remember writing this? It feels like writing to a different person - you are me though! Just remember that once upon time you were me and we were worrying about the future.

Today I worry about how my parents are going to freak out when I tell them that I decided to not follow their religion. Instead I want to connect to God in a different way. I want to take a break from the arduous rituals that I enjoyed at one time. However now, I want to live with my spirit and allow my heart to sing.

I've looked at many spiritual classes at the local spiritual center and there are so many that I want to take. I will decide soon. In the meantime, I have been praying, journaling, meditating and using affirmations. I feel so much better keeping my attitude positive. However I know there is more work to be done. I am learning and growing each day, the more I connect with myself using my spiritual tools.

I need to get over the hurdle with my parents. They are so strict with tradition and religion. I know this is going to break their hearts. However my heart is breaking, and I need to make changes for me. Time is precious so I plan to take the opportunity while I have time to make changes.

I feel sick. My stomach feels sick. I am a bundle of nerves. This is all I think about. I need to see the light at the end of the tunnel. I know it's there but I can't quite see it. My parents are going to be so upset.

I hope you're doing well. If not, don't worry because everything will turn out for the best. It only gets better each day.

Never stop dreaming. You have the tenacity and drive to get where you want to be. You have passion fueled by your spirit. I will check in again soon. Good luck!
Love, Me of March 2010

The bottom line is to unwind the old beliefs and wind in peace, love and joy for yourself. When you heal yourself, you heal the world around you. It starts with you. You're the teacher by setting and living the example. When you go with your spirit, you can't go wrong!

‖‖

EXERCISES

Be who you are and say what you feel because those who mind don't matter and those who matter don't mind.
—Dr. Seuss

How many times have you said to yourself, "I should have listened to my gut?" Your gut always knows. What feeling have you been getting in your gut for a while concerning spirituality? What are these feelings or nudges urging you to become more aware of?

_____

_____

_____

_____

_____

List 4 ways your life will be more positive when you connect with your spirituality.

1. _____

2. _____

3. _____

4. _____

List 4 positive things you will have by staying in your current religion or not living your life spiritually.

1. _____

2. _____

3. _____

4. _____

Answer the following questions honestly:
What do I fear most about religion?

_____

What is my greatest fear with my parents, family, friends, community, and other relationships?

_____

What am I getting from this religion?

_____

What do I fear will happen if I let go of this religion?

_____

Do I deserve to be happy in my spirituality?

_____

Am I willing to let go and be free?

_____

Bonus: Download free exercises, meditations, tips, etc. at
www.TinaSacchi.com

Notes

Chapter 15

Guilt Has a
Low Vibration

Dismiss whatever insults your soul.
—Walt Whitman

Guilt Breeds Irrational Thought

*I*n spite of all my personal and spiritual growth and my desire to find my authentic spiritual self– even with meditation and personal inquiries – I was still feeling an enormous amount of guilt about leaving behind the religion of my birth, my family, my culture, my ancestry. The guilt weighed me down inside, so heavy, dark, and gloomy. I think some of the burden came from feeling I was carrying the guilt not only for myself, but for my ancestors' sake, as well. An ancient pattern was trying to continue its passage down through the generations. I had been conditioned by my parents, who had been conditioned by theirs – back who knows how many hundreds or thousands of years – to believe a certain way. The pressure to live up to this responsibility was grueling. No wonder I experienced the feeling of doing something wrong, that I had failed my obligation to my religious duties.

Worst of all was that nagging thought that God would punish me if I didn't carry on these beliefs and traditions. Even though I knew, intellectually, that God does not punish us like that, the distressing doubt lingered. I was letting my family down, so was I disappointing God, too? And if he was disappointed, didn't he have a right to punish me? It was irrational thought, but powerfully disturbing, nonetheless.

We all go through different phases in our lives. There are times when we feel low, down and depressed. Other times we feel high on life where everything is wonderful and full of unlimited possibilities. The difference is in our vibration. Guilt is a low vibration and therefore you may have a hard time connecting and seeing any aspect of the Divine or God if you are feeling guilty. But when you're free of guilt, the whole world glows with Divine light. To connect with your authentic spiritual self, it's best to be in a higher vibration. Since guilt has a very low vibrational energy, I knew I absolutely had to get rid of mine. And fast.

Eventually, I determined that the only way I could deal with the guilt was by chipping away at it, peeling back one emotion at a time. And I had to undertake this process on my own. Nevertheless, although I was alone physically, I knew my spiritual guides and angels would be right there to assist me. I was reassured by their love, comfort, compassion, guidance, direction, and help … I had it all from them. Most importantly, I had faith!

I kept hearing the words:

Follow your heart. Follow your spirit. You can't go wrong when you do so. If you listen to your mind, the biggest party pooper in town, you will stray from your path. Sing, love, fly, dance, laugh, and rejoice your spirituality. Everything will work out. There is no other way. Don't look back. What's in the past is in the past. It didn't work for you, so you're going in a new direction. We are here to help. Just ask and we will guide you. Don't worry about the 'how.' That is our job. Just take the next step. Have trust and faith in the process.

One Step at a Time

All this guidance was unimaginable – it seemed so easy to hear such comforting words from them. But how was I supposed to get my head out of the way? I had spent years in school using my head. My MBA was proof. Working in corporate America, I'd had to use my head or I'd have been out of a job. There had been neither time nor tolerance for using my imagination or my spirituality during those years. So now, with more than 30 years of schooling and work experience using my head, I was being guided to do the exact opposite. Trust? Faith? Take one step at a time! I'd been used to 5- and 10-year budget and business plans – now I was being told those things were all unnecessary. Really?

In spite of my head overanalyzing all these new thoughts and ideas, my heart and spirit were roaring with trust and faith. I **had** to move on! There were no other options. I was done working and living with dis-eases. It was time to make a change. And simple, too. Just take the next step. I was tentative, to be sure, but I did it. I took a class on living your heart's desires through spirituality. How refreshing! And once I'd taken that class, I signed up for another class, and then another and another and another. I had surrounded myself with like-minded people, and now I joined groups that encouraged my new spiritual life. My spirit was flying high and I was truly happy.

But with the happiness came a challenge, for the more I connected with my spirit through all I was learning, the more I had to face my fears about whether to stay in or come out of my spiritual closet. I knew that soon I would just have to come out. I had faith and trusted that it would happen naturally and spiritually. That was my goal and desire. So I continued to follow my heart and spirit, along with the advice of my guides and angels.

And my coming out did happen spiritually, if in a very unique way. It unfolded over time, with the assistance of those special ingredients, faith and trust. The more I connected to my spirituality, the more my true feelings surfaced. An inner song was developing in my soul. I was shocked that living my spiritual truth could produce such a sweet melody. This song kept me on track. Soon, I noticed a skip in my step, a twinkle in my heart, and a wagging tail. I continued to experience the feeling that spirituality was pure, simple joy. This was my interpretation of the signs. And my beliefs and experience were all that mattered.

I was released from the burden of feeling I should follow an ancestral belief from thousands of years ago. Thought it perhaps made sense then, it didn't make sense today, especially not for me. My song boosted my confidence more and more each moment, each day, each year.

Going to Hell in a Hand-basket

A client, Trina, was having difficulty sleeping. Her insomnia was causing many problems, such as foggy memory, lack of focus, irritability, and anger. She'd toss and turn all night, and just as she'd finally fall asleep, it would be time to get up and go to work. Needless to say, her work performance was affected and her chances for a promotion were in serious jeopardy. She'd simply had enough.

"How long has sleeplessness been going on?" I asked.

"For about a year, now," Trina replied.

"What kinds of changes have occurred during this time?" I asked.

"I really can't think of anything," Trina said. "My children are doing great in school. My husband is successful with his business. Everything is fine, and I am grateful for my life, but I am so frustrated because the lack of sleep is driving me crazy!"

I prodded deeper. "Have there been any activities, friends, or relationship changes over the last few years?"

"Well, yes. I used to be more involved at church. Now I don't go as often, if at all. My kids don't want to attend and my husband has never cared for it, so we pretty much stopped going," she replied.

"How do you feel about that?" I asked.

"Well, part of me feels like I am OK without going, but there definitely is a part of me that misses it," Trina explained.

"What do you miss about it?" I inquired.

"I miss the social aspect of it. Since we've stopped going, I haven't had a chance to see old friends."

"If your children and husband had an interest in going, would you be happy attending?" I asked.

"Wow, I guess I never thought of it that way. I really feel I have nothing in common with that church any longer. It doesn't fill me the way it used to, especially that fearful part," Trina said.

"Tell me about the fearful part," I gently nudged.

"Well, the minister always tells us that if we don't follow the rules of the religion, we will all go to hell. I really don't see it that way anymore. My friends and family still believe that, but I don't. And when we get together, they often remind me that since I am no longer attending services, I am going to hell. They also tell me they are praying for me and praying for my salvation," Trina explained.

At that point, it was very clear to me that although Trina had outgrown her religion, subconsciously, she had programs running that were still giving these beliefs validity.

Over subsequent weeks, we proceeded to deprogram her subconscious mind, using various alternative healing techniques such as hypnotherapy, energy healing, and affirmations and other tools I shared with you in Chapter 13. As a result, Trina is sleeping through the night. Zzzzzzzz…

Confront Guilt Head-On

Confronting guilt head-on is a great way to diffuse it and diminish its power. When you start to sense the guilt rising, just allow yourself to feel it. Let the sensation run through your mind, body, spirit, and emotions. Notice where it lodges in your body. Some people feel guilt in the pit of their stomachs. From a metaphysical standpoint, this is the emotional powerhouse. The feeling is due to the fact that you are allowing someone else to take your power. Others feel guilt in their emotional body, and tears flow. This is a great release, so allow them to fall. Clear all the guilt out of your system. However, take care not to allow it to seep back in and again take up residence there. With intention, allow other feelings like peace, love, joy, and self-respect to take its place. Allow the guilt to run its course or it will come back more powerfully the next time you experience a trigger.

After allowing the guilt to flow out, do something that makes you feel good, something soothing and relaxing like affirmations, meditation, bathing, gardening, scrapbooking, reading, writing, journaling, or playing golf, tennis, or another sport. Use affirmations such as, "I allow myself to believe what I want to believe," to fill your being with calming, nurturing energy.

A Step-by-Step Guide to Conquering Guilt

Following this twelve step program will help you release some of your guilt as you move forward in your spiritual emancipation.

1. **Figure out whether you believe in a higher power**. Really pay attention to your feelings regarding where you stand in this belief. What you believe now may be different than what you were taught, but there is no right or wrong. In fact, it's the belief that there are right and wrong beliefs that leads to guilt. But that's not from God. Things are what they are, guilt-free. Presumably you have some belief in a higher power, since you are reading this book about living a spiritual life. However, you were conditioned to think a certain way and now that differs from your new point of view, so you need to diminish the power of that early (or lifelong) conditioning. You no longer believe your new thoughts are bad, evil, or sinful. But start small.

2. **Skip a service or two**, and then note that nothing terrible happens when you do.

3. **Pray your own way**, rather than the way you were taught, and again realize that nothing bad happens … or maybe great things happen, like more peace and contentment in your life since you're now following your inner guidance. It gets easier and easier as you take small steps toward your spirituality. Meditation, chanting and singing are all forms of praying. As a matter of fact, I always say that *singing is praying twice*!

4. **Read everything you can get your hands on.** With information right at our fingertips – via books, publications, the Internet, forums, etc. – you can easily read how others are finding ways to work through their religious quandaries. The more you do this, the more you will realize that even though your religion may be different from theirs, a LOT of people are experiencing the same kind of religious guilt caused by friends and family members and are learning how to resolve it. Moreover, you will find that you are not alone. The power of religious upbringing is astonishingly strong, and in certain situations, it can be a form of brainwashing. If you feel guilty for thinking differently than your clan, it's time to just take the next step on discovering your true path.. . .

5. **Assess your situation candidly.** Take control and release your guilt by following your heart, not your head. Your head will lead you to guilt; your heart will lead you to your passion.

6. **Talk to people about various religions and listen to their views and feedback.** Celebrate your differences and enhance your interfaith communication. Recognize that there are lots of differences among humans. It is natural for people to have different preferences when it comes to food, clothing, interests ... and even religions. I have never met two people—even from the same family and religious upbringing—who agree 100 percent on everything, Take time to learn about the various religious holidays that occur throughout the year. This knowledge will help you understand how others live and can serve as a guide for how you want to live. Talking to others will help you find your place without the unnecessary guilt that was instilled

in you over your lifetime. You will gain knowledge and knowledge is power. And remember, to learn new things is not a sin! It's educational!

7. **Attend various religious services and learn about different faiths.** Observing other religions will help you understand others' beliefs and confirm your new way of thinking. This is very helpful when it comes to discovering whether or not you're missing anything. It's also helpful to simply discover what is right for you.

8. **Give yourself permission to take a break!** If you feel that you've simply had enough from religion and need a break to figure it out, then go easy on yourself. Nothing bad will happen to you. You are not going to go to hell! You are fine just the way you are. When you don't know what your next step is, just hang out and wait. When you do so, you open yourself to becoming aware of opportunities and possibilities. If you force the situation and try too hard to belong to something, you block yourself from your path and cannot fully show up to whatever is at hand.

9. **Know that God loves you regardless of whether you are attending service.** He knows that you're trying to decipher and integrate your religious and spiritual views.

10. **Seek out the professionals!** Certain religious issues are very deep, and you might require help to get you through them. This is not a sign of weakness. There is nothing wrong with talking things out with someone who's an expert at helping you for your highest good. Talking about your feelings can help you see them from a different perspective and often assists you to deal with them more easily.

11. **Keep a journal.** Record all of your revelations, insights, discoveries, feelings, etc. You will be able to refer to this at a later time for comfort or recall.

12. **Cut the cords to guilt and shame.** The more you feel disconnected from God or your spirituality, the more guilt and shame you will experience. It's imperative that you start from within and connect spiritually in your own special way. At prayer time, after opening up your sacred space, ask God and your guardian angels to help you cut all cords that are not for your highest good, especially the religious cords that are connected to guilt and shame. Imagine severing them with the energy of love, light, peace, and joy. Then fill yourself up with this energy, as well. Record your experience in your journal.

And One Final Helpful Tool

In the beginning, my family would throw accusations my way, and I would defend myself in kind, throwing accusations back at them. We got nowhere. These were among the most unpleasant times in my life. I dreaded to see or be near any of them.

Then I started to role play responses in my mind, in the mirror, and with my colleagues. Role playing allowed me practice and the opportunity to rehearse my responses many times. With each role playing session came different questions and emotions that I discovered and worked through. This activity helped me unwind the old beliefs and stories that were once part of who I was. It also helped me see that I was ready to let go.

To role play, ask a supportive friend to assume the role of a person who will have objections to your choices. Prepare your friend in advance with potential objections.

Prepare answers to some objections that you may get. Note that the other person's emotions will come through with each statement/question. The more you do this, the more comfortable you will be if you choose to go to the person who is challenging you, or if that person approaches you first you will be prepared. Your subconscious will be creating a record of responses and answers.

Remember that we all want to be loved and honored so it is very important to show love and honor as you share your desires with your objecting loved one. Further, assure them that their guidance to date has been invaluable, and you will always cherish their love, but you are here to figure this out on your own. What you would like is their support, for them to be there for you.

Always start your reply with something positive about the other person. This may not turn their strict, embedded, concrete ways, but you will diffuse something on an intangible level. Hopefully if the person hears it often enough, his or her subconscious will anchor these suggestions, and in due time he or she may come around and meet you somewhere in the middle, if not all the way.

- I love you, ...
- You are the greatest, ...
- I honor you, ...

For instance, you may say:

- You are a great parent, I love you, and I need to take a break from church.
- You are a great person, I love you, and I decided not to baptize my kids.

- You are a great parent, I love and honor you, and I am giving up the ministry.

Here is how this might work in a real conversation:

"How dare you do this?"

"You are a great parent, I love you, and I need to take a break from church."

"How long a break?"

"I love you especially for caring about me and I don't know how long. I am taking a break."

"How can you do this to me?"

"I honor you and love you. I was asking the same thing of myself. How can I do this to myself, to continue when my heart isn't in it?"

"Someone is influencing you! It's your friend isn't it? I knew she was no good!"

"I want to let you know how much I love you, and I need to love myself the same way. I am deciding by myself. No one is telling me what to do."

And on it goes. . .

Remember this dialogue may continue for a minute, an hour, days, weeks, or years. You are simply stating that your love hasn't changed for them (unless it has), and that you are deciding to change direction. In fact, this same dialogue with the same questions may come up over and over again. In that case, remain as calm, cool and collected as you can. Otherwise you will be adding more fuel to the fire.

As I practiced role playing over time, I noticed that when the religion subject came up from time to time, my family was looking for fire from me, but there was none. They would begin their attacks fuming at me, and I responded calmly with no animosity, accusations or anger as if I were saying,

"I am wearing my sneakers today." Over time, as they tried and got no bite, I could actually see them calming down since I didn't meet them at their tension level. The daily wars that had continued for a long time were now reduced to skirmishes every so often. They would test me indirectly to see if I changed my mind about church and all the beliefs that go along with it. For instance, my mom still attends church and makes a point of telling me that. I respond cool as a cucumber, "That's great mom. What did you learn today from the priest?" She goes on to tell me, and I hold space and listen because I am truly honoring her beliefs with the hope that she will do the same and honor me. Though we may never see eye-to-eye, we have come a long way from war to co-existence. I know that serenity and peace start with me and that if I hadn't honored my spirit and moved in its direction, I would be unhappy today and wouldn't even be writing this book.

Be sure to refrain from blaming others for your predicament and for your guilt. Many people are doing the best they can with what they know and are capable of accomplishing. Some are still asleep. You have received your wake up call and you have awakened, so it's celebration time—time to move on with your heart and spirit. For others, the awakening may come later. Have compassion toward them.

||||||||||||||||||||||||||||||||||||||||||||||||||||

EXERCISES

The lesson which life repeats and constantly enforces is 'look under foot.' You are always nearer the divine and the true sources of power than you think.

— John Burroughs

List the steps you can take to eliminate religious guilt.

_____

_____

_____

_____

Role play in your journal. Write your possible responses to the following objections family members may raise:

Objection: You are disrespecting me.

Possible response: You are a great person, I love you and respect you highly and I want you to know that.

You are disrespecting the family.

_____

_____

You are disrespecting our religion.

_____

_____

You are disrespecting our community.

_____

_____

You are dishonoring me.

_____

_____

You are dishonoring the family.

_____

_____

You are dishonoring our religion.

_____

_____

How can you hurt me this way?

_____

_____

How can you do this to me?

_____

_____

I will disown you if you do this.

_____

_____

You will no longer be part of this family.

_____

_____

We will write you out of the will.

_____

_____

You will rot in hell if you do this.

_____

_____

God will punish you.

_____

_____

God will punish me and the rest of the family.

_____

_____

Bad luck will be in your life.

_____

_____

Bad luck will be in my life.

_____

_____

If you do this, I don't ever want to see you again.

_____

_____

List other religions you might have an interest in learning about.

_____

_____

_____

_____

Now go ahead and read about them. Attend services. Try them on for size.

What are some affirmations you can use to reinforce releasing the guilt and embracing a free, new spiritual path?

_____

_____

_____

Avoid dwelling on the past, since that is a complete waste of time. Simply acknowledge past events and move on. List some ways to celebrate answering your spiritual wake-up call.

_____

_____

_____

_____

Don't hesitate to seek out a professional if you need help dealing with the guilt you're experiencing. List some specific issues a professional could help you work through?

_____

_____

_____

_____

Bonus: Download free exercises, meditations, tips, etc. at
*www.**TinaSacchi**.com*
||||||||||||||||||||||||||||||||||||||||||||||||||||

Notes

Chapter 16

All We Need Is Love

"We have just enough religion to make us hate, but not enough to make us love one another. "
—Jonathan Swift

"You're Pushing My Buttons Again!"

When someone is pushing your buttons, it's really not them pushing your buttons. You are pushing your own buttons. In fact, feeling that your buttons are being pushed is really an indication that your spirit is trying to communicate with you that this is your next lesson in loving unconditionally. This lesson is twofold: learning the actual lesson and then removing the emotional reaction or charge in order to reclaim your inner power. When you think that someone continues to trigger a charge in you, you are giving your time and energy away to them by constantly thinking, talking, and even dreaming about the experience It's important to keep in mind that you have a choice to continue to be charged and give away your energy or learn what part of you needs healing so you can progress. This is a perfect opportunity to reclaim your energy, love, and move on to something else.

The bottom-line in living a spiritual life is to love yourself as well as others unconditionally. So what is it that prevents you from loving unconditionally in every situation? If your buttons are pushed, it basically means that there are more lessons on unconditional love to be learned. What would God do in your case? He would love! So what will it take you to love them too?

Again, you may be saying, "That's easier said than done!" However, I know you can do it. Your spirit presents you with challenges all the time. What matters is how you handle and learn from them. Have you ever heard the line that positive people live in a positive world and negative people live in a negative world? How can that be if it's all one world? The difference is in our perception and what each of us chooses to do regarding the issue at hand. Is it possible that positive people are excelling in loving others unconditionally because they work on their perception? That positive people are seeing others through God's eyes?

Years ago I believed that others used to deliberately push my buttons, and since I felt emotionally distraught I blamed my sadness or hurt on them. It was all their fault for making me feel so bad. Now when I see that my buttons are being pushed, I tap into spirit using spiritual tools. I release the charge by seeing through God's eyes and reaching an understanding that when we are looking at others, we are also looking at God since we are all connected.

Of course, certain situations take me longer to resolve than others. Each time I think I have accomplished the lesson, I check by viewing the situation through God's eyes and discern

I my feelings. If my feelings are still charged then I know there is more to work on or more layers to peel away. Once my feelings are neutral then I know I can move on. I will always have the memory of the situation; but, there is no longer an emotional reaction. As I continued to transform myself, I began to live spiritually. However, if I had remained in judgment mode, it would have been impossible for me to evolve; I would have become stagnant and stuck in place. One day I was explaining to my son that his action toward me created a discontentment within me. He looked at me puzzled. I later learned that his quizzical look meant, "How can she let this get to her?" And so I kept explaining to him what he did and how it made me feel. He finally responded: "I don't know what you are talking about and I don't care." He then completely removed himself from the situation and walked away singing and playing in a different part of the house without attachment especially without giving his energy away. I realized at that moment that he had a deep unconditional love for himself and he loved me. However he wasn't the one pushing the buttons. He knew this innately. It wasn't his stuff and so he walked away.

I always access that memory from my subconscious mind when I need to walk away from something that is consciously ridiculous for me to continuously hash over. Thanks son, for being a superb teacher of unconditional love.

The Spiritual Frontline

We often fail to realize that the people who push our buttons are some of our greatest spiritual teachers. Our spirits set us up for battle. Not only that but we are also learning lessons. What a huge responsibility! Imagine your spirit setting you up out on the frontline so that you can be attacked by others because they perceive you differently than you really are or intend to be?

This has been one of the biggest challenges in my life: my parents, who come from a different culture and belief system, have always tried to instill their beliefs in me, and they would get angry and resentful when I would resist. For many decades I thought they were deliberately pushing my buttons. I would always complain about them, "If only they could be open and see things my way! How could they be so close-minded and hold onto their outmoded, old-world views?"

It was only as I did more personal development work and continued to grow spiritually that I realized I was the one who wasn't really open. I thought that since I had a more worldly view, I was open – but, in fact, I was not. I didn't act the way God would. That is to honor my parents' level of understanding and perception and love them unconditionally at the same time. Once I realized this, I started to be able to see life through their eyes. My perception changed, so I changed.

This doesn't mean I started to live according to their rules and beliefs; however the conflicts no longer mattered. The cat-and-mouse arguments disappeared. Of course, there were times when they tried to instigate arguments; those were the times my spirit was tested, but the sparks were gone. Over and over again they would ask me about church and why I wasn't attending? Or why my kids were not attending religious education? Or why I didn't follow through with certain religious practices? In the beginning, I was irritated with all these questions. How dare they keep insisting and imposing their beliefs on me I would say and feel. Later, as I worked through it by trying to see their perspective and releasing my attachments to their beliefs, I stood my ground lovingly, and calmly assured that the good news is that I pray and connect to God in my own special way. And although it is obvious they don't agree with me even up to this day, I don't add fuel to the fire by being upset or angry when subtly they drop hints or ask questions.

When there is no fuel, there is no fire. My parents may have tried to instigate a fight, but they end up hearing themselves talk. I don't give them any spark since there isn't any. And so eventually they stop, and the conversation is magically dropped. We went on to talk about common interests.

Another remarkable thing happened as I changed my perception: my parents started changing, too. They lightened up in many aspects of their lives. Their defensive attitudes toward religion lessened each time we came together. It wasn't even in the forefront of our meetings anymore. And as we all put less and less emphasis on it, we were able to have a lighter and more enjoyable time together. That is not to say that we believe the same way, for there is still much more to learn. However, when you heal yourself, you really do heal the world around you.

Although it sometimes may not look or feel like it, everyone is really just trying to do the best they can. Like the old saying goes, unless you walk in someone's shoes for a mile, you cannot understand where that person has been or what they're up against. When we're busy judging others, we stop examining our own behavior, growth, and evolution! And that means we are procrastinating in our self-development and stunting our spiritual growth.

So the next time you notice your buttons being pushed, say to yourself, "Terrific! It's spiritual lesson time. Let me learn the lessons, and move on!"

Released from Pain

Sarah, a beautiful woman in her mid 40s, came to me complaining of pain all over her body. She had been dealing with this pain for many years, but just couldn't handle it any longer and decided to do some alternative healing. This totally went against the teachings of her religion: she had been born and raised a Mormon. Sarah had tremendous guilt even making the appointment.

The first thing she said was, "If they find out that I'm going outside the church for healing, I'll be punished. However, something is telling me that this is what I need to do."

I assured her that in my practice everyone is entitled to his or her own free will, and there wouldn't be any negative consequences.

"Free will?" she asked. "What is that?"

I explained my belief that anyone can decide what is appropriate for his or her own spirit.

"Anyone?" she asked.

"Yes, anyone. As a matter of fact, I want to encourage you to tap into your spirit to determine what is best for your highest good."

"Well, how do you do that?"

"You've already done it. Didn't you just tell me that something was telling you that making this appointment was what you needed to do?"

"Oh, yes," she replied.

"Well, your spirit was nudging you to take a path of healing rather than a path of judgment and consequences." Right there I could see her brighten up.

Sarah secretly came to me for several more alternative healing sessions, and the progress that transpired was unbelievable. Every physical ailment has an emotional source that breeds the dis-ease. In Sarah's situation, her spirit felt immobilized, restricted, paralyzed, even crippled. The more she tapped into her spirit, allowing it to guide her, the further she reduced her pain. The less pain she experienced, the more rapidly her self-confidence grew.

A few months later, Sarah called to joyfully report her new accomplishments. She had helped some people in her community transition out of their restrictive religion by connecting with their spirits. She was the perfect guide for them because she understood where they were coming from and where they were headed. There wasn't a better person than Sarah to assist them.

||||||||||||||||||||||||||||||||||||||||||||||||||||||

EXERCISES

Be careful how you interpret the world. It is like that.
—Erich Heller

What can you do to embrace life's lessons when you feel others are "pushing your buttons"?

_____

_____

_____

_____

_____

There are spiritual reasons we were born into a certain family, religion, culture, and environment. Many of these have to do with the lessons we came to learn in this lifetime. What are some of the reasons you think you were born into your family, religion, culture, or environment?

_____

_____

_____

_____

How can your experiences help you grow in your understanding and compassion so that you can (a) appreciate those who have different perspectives from your own and (b) help others who may be in the same situation?

_____

_____

_____

How can you view your experiences and memories as blessings, and then move on?

_____

_____

_____

Bonus: Download free exercises, meditations, tips, etc. at
*www.**TinaSacchi**.com*

Notes

Chapter 17

What Would God Do?

When we seek to discover the best in others,
we somehow bring out the best in ourselves.
—William Arthur Ward

"The moment we judge others, we are judging ourselves because we are looking in the mirror." One of my mentors said this to me decades ago, and I really didn't understand it then. Occasionally, I would think about her comment, but it still didn't make sense. It was something I had to learn over time.

"How can we be looking in the mirror if we're watching somebody else doing something wrong?" I asked her.

In answer, she asked me, "Why is what they're doing wrong?"

"Because people are supposed to act a certain way," I remember saying in response.

"According to whose rules?" she prodded, further.

"Under society's rules!" I said, sure I was right.

"Well, do you think all societies believe the same way?" she upped the ante.

"No, probably not," I admitted.

Then, a great deal of time passed before I read the following:

> *We don't see things as they are.*
> *We see things as we are.*
> — Anais Nin

And then I got it! You know what they say, that it all makes sense when you're ready to hear it. I now understood the meaning of my mentor's words.

When you are in judgment, you're looking into a mirror. Once you accept that fact, the next step is to ask yourself what you need from this person by requiring them to act a certain way. Chances are it's a need or desire you must fulfill within yourself.

Here are some common judgments we hear (or say) all the time:

I am fat.
She's unfriendly.
He's so abrupt.
She's very selfish.
He's ugly!
I am stupid.
He's so mean.
She's the slowest cashier!
He only goes to religious services a few times a year, so he's going to hell.

What kind of mother is she?!
How can she wear that color blouse with those pants?
He's too skinny.
She's had too much plastic surgery.
She needs plastic surgery.
Look at that beer belly on him!
He's acting so strange – he must be on drugs.

She needs an attitude adjustment.	She's a terrible driver.
	Who does he think he is?!
He's so closed-minded.	She's weird and off the wall.

If you're negative, you see only negative characteristics. When you're positive, the glass is half full. It's that simple! As soon as you change your thoughts ... poof ... the world you see becomes different. So how do you accomplish that?

Transforming Judgment

When you are judging, you are not seeing through God's eyes. You are condemning, criticizing, dooming, and connecting with a lower vibration and as a result you move away from living a spiritual life. However, if you're looking toward developing a spiritual life, it is wise to divest yourself of judgment. This can be a challenge, particularly if you've been at the judgment game for quite some time. It's especially difficult if you try to do it alone or without any help. This is a time when Divine assistance can really come in handy. Any time you find yourself making a judgment about somebody or yourself, ask God to help you transform that thought or judgment. Then ask God to enhance it.

||||||||||||||||||||||||||||||||||||||||||||||||||||||||||

Anytime you find yourself in judgment, whether it's about yourself or someone else, say:

God please transform this thought.
God please enhance this thought.

||||||||||||||||||||||||||||||||||||||||||||||||||||||||||

For example:

You think: She is nasty and unfriendly! (God please transform this thought)

You say: *"She has a giving quality."* God please enhance this thought.

You think: He's so closed minded about religious doctrine. (God please transform this thought)

You say: His belief in God is so honorable. (God please enhance this thought)

You think: My parents are wrong and so critical of my spiritual beliefs. (God please transform this thought)

You say: My parents want the very best for me and I honor them for that. (God please enhance this thought)

I challenge you to consciously use this exercise from this moment on and notice how it changes your perception. This is a great way to shift the energy around your judgment. You will notice that your life changes almost instantly as you become more consciously and unconsciously aware

Jesus was a particularly good example of living without judgment. Taking his lead, it is our spiritual obligation to give others the benefit of the doubt. Whenever you experience any doubt about how to transform a judgment, ask yourself: *What would God do in my place?*

The answer will always be: ***Love them!***

Hold Space for Others, But…

This non-judgment idea may sound good … but you may have a hard time understanding where some people are coming from.

Trust me, I understand because I have been there!

So what can you do? First of all, you must find a way to relate to your parents or other religious people who are challenging you without the lens of judgment coloring how you see them. It may help to realize that for them religion is a good thing, even if it doesn't work for you. These may be very intelligent people, which may be part of why you find their seemingly antiquated beliefs so hard to understand. From their perspective, their religion represents doing the right thing and provides guidance for how to approach all of life. Yes, there are downsides, like the guilt – but even guilt can have positive results. It can encourage one to work harder, be faithful to one's spouse, or stay out of debt, for example.

Non-judgment won't be an automatic cure-all. There will still be people who disagree with you. All you can do for them is to continue to love them. No need to judge or disagree. Doing so will only distract you from your mission and take you off task.

Remember, it's all a process. Take baby steps, one step at a time, until you can plow forward.

Training for the Rat Race

When Janice, a college student, came to me, she was at her wits' end. "My parents are always criticizing my academics," she said.

"What is your GPA?" I asked.

"It's 3.9."

"Wow, that's great!"

"Tell that to my parents," Janice lamented. "They don't seem to think so."

"Really? What do they expect your grades to be?"

"A 4.0, and they think I should be President of the Marketing Club, rather than Vice President. They also want me to be fluent in many languages, but Tina, I just don't like studying languages. My Spanish class is what brought my GPA down to a 3.9."

"Why is it important to them that you learn various languages?"

"The world is changing so much today. They think it will give me a better chance at a more competitive position, since most kids are only studying one foreign language."

"Is that something you believe? Do you think that the only way to get a job you love is by speaking several languages?"

"What do you mean by 'job I love'?"

That stopped me for a moment. "Well, Janice," I continued slowly, "what would be your idea of an ideal job, something you'd really like to do?"

Janice's face lit up. "I want to get a well-paying position using my marketing skills."

"In any specific area?"

"Oh, any area would be good," she said, still animated.

"So you're telling that if you got a well-paying position marketing cigarettes, you would be happy to accept it?"

"Cigarettes? No, I wouldn't want a job in that industry. I don't believe in smoking, so that wouldn't be a job I'd be interested in," Janice explained.

"Really? Even if it were a high-paying position where you could win all sorts of bonuses, you would not take a job marketing cigarettes?"

"No. I would not be in my integrity if I did so. I'm not interested in pursuing a career that would take me in that direction," she answered.

"You're right, Janice, you wouldn't. And it sounds to me like **you** have the final say about which direction you want to take with your career. So why are you allowing yourself to become distraught over something you don't want to do and have no interest in?"

"Well, if I learn more languages, I'll have a better chance of landing a good job," she said, repeating and defending her family's line.

"Maybe. However, you told me you are not interested in languages, so that is a direction you wouldn't want to take," I changed course. "Whose belief is it that learning more languages will get you a higher paying position? Yours or your parents?"

"It must be mine, Tina, otherwise it wouldn't be bothering me so much," Janice admitted. "Wait … I get it! I got stuck believing this was the only way for me to find a good job. But first I need to love what I am doing! And it's not really about getting a high-paying job – it's about doing what I love!"

"You just won Spiritual BINGO," I told Janice. "Congratulate yourself, because many people don't get it this early in their lives."

Janice's awareness was the start for coming to terms with her parents' judgment as well as her own self-judgment. I helped her design and create a pathway for her passion and vision and as a result, she had a plan with confidence and enthusiasm. Her parents warmed up to her, noticing these fine qualities in her and became supportive.

||||||||||||||||||||||||||||||||||||||||||||||||||||||

EXERCISES
If you judge people, you have no time to love them.
— Mother Teresa

What are some of the judgments you regularly make about other people regarding religion and/or spirituality?

_____

_____

_____

What kinds of judgments do you regularly make about yourself regarding religion and/or spirituality?

_____

_____

_____

_____

What's in it for you to be judgmental?

_____

_____

_____

_____

_____

If you're honest, are the judgments you're making about other people really things you want to work on yourself? What can you do to become more aware of these judgments?

_____

_____

_____

_____

_____

How can you transform the judgments into helpful, positive statements?

_____

_____

_____

_____

_____

How will you enhance these judgments?

_____

_____

_____

_____

Bonus: Download free exercises, meditations, tips, etc. at
*www.**TinaSacchi**.com*
|||||||||||||||||||||||||||||||||||||||||||||||||||||

Notes

Notes

Part Four

Staying On Spiritual Task.... Spiritual Maintenance for a Spiritual Lifestyle

Chapter 18:

Connect with Your Divine Support Team

"A man may be the greatest philosopher in the world but a child in religion. When a man has developed a high state of spirituality he can understand that the kingdom of heaven is within him."
—Swami Vivekananda

We all have a Divine Support Team. When I finally got this, there was a sense of freedom, a sense that I was not alone. I often tell my students and clients that we came from God before we came into the world as we humanly know it. And just because we came here, God doesn't say: "Okay my dear; you're on your own now. I will leave you to yourself and good luck." This would be absurd. Instead we have many spiritual beings as helpers. We can call upon them at any time. Whether they are angels, guides, or spirits we have resources. We simply call upon them for help and they are there. It's so simple. They cannot interfere with our free will. This was a lesson I had to learn the longer way.

When I decided to come out of the spiritual closet, I needed to work through many issues such as friends disagreeing with me and with my beliefs. People thought I was odd since I believed in the "woo-woo" stuff. They thought I was strange and confused. Strange—not. However, I was confused.

I believed in angels, but they were not instantaneously there to help me. What gives? I kept meditating over and over again, communicating with them and telling them that I needed help. Why did they not appear to rescue me? They kept repeating the annoying statement over and over again. "We can't interfere with your freewill."

I would respond, "Please do. I need your help 24/7. Where are you when I need you?" Again they responded that they could not interfere.

Well this was really making me angry. One day I was livid, but I decided to calm down and meditate deeper in order to have a one-on-one with my guardian angel. My guardian angel added, "If we interfere with your freewill, then we will be living your life. You need to live your own life. We will come to you when you ask us."

At that point I got it–reluctantly. However I got it. I say "reluctantly" because I am the type of person that wants to get things done as efficiently as possible, and being efficient means there should be an understanding that help is always appreciated. However, this spirituality thing was still new to me and I decided to go for it. From then on, I invited my angels everywhere I went, every move I made, every time I thought of them. They were always invited. I realized how much easier my life became. I felt their comfort, guidance, whispers, touch, enlightenment, teachings, etc. I felt it all.

I was truly amazed on how easy it was. I simply had to invite them in and there they were. I also learned that when I was done with them, I had to release them and express gratitude. I thanked them. Wow! That was it!

The Answers are There, But You've Got to Listen

Jennifer came to me one day for spiritual career coaching. She wanted to move out of accounting and do something more exciting with her life. She said, "You know Tina, I pray and pray, but I never get any answers to my prayers."

At that moment, her spirit guide showed up. He informed me that he did answer Jennifer's prayers, but she didn't listen to the answers. As a matter of fact, she didn't want the answers he'd given, and so she dismissed them.

"Jennifer I believe that you're praying," I said, "but are you listening to the answers?"

"Well I try," she said "but I don't get any."

"Your spirit guide is telling me that he has placed certain thoughts in your head. These are your answers. Does this make sense for you?"

"Well, I don't think I've been getting them." Jennifer persisted.

"He is telling me that working with animals is part of your life purpose. Does this resonate with you?"

"Yes it does," she responded with excitement. "As matter of fact, I keep seeing dogs and cats around me. I am at peace when I'm around animals. I feel real happy every time I go by the veterinarian hospital near my house. I sometimes have the urge to go in but I don't."

"So what you're telling me is that you've been getting messages about your purpose as well as feelings and emotions associated with them right?"

"I guess so," Jennifer said.

"So how did you expect to receive this message Jennifer? Through an email, telegram or postal service?"

We both chuckled. "You know Tina you're right. I probably thought it had to be this big thing; the sky would open and down would come my answer, my purpose."

"Well you know it was sort of like that Jennifer. You were the antenna to receive all this guidance. However you dismissed it. You expected for it to be different when, in fact, it was not what you're accustomed to."

"It feels real good regarding animals," Jennifer continued. "I am totally thrilled. However how do I do that? I cannot leave my current job since I make good money."

"Now that is a different story," I replied. "For today we found your purpose. We will work on the next steps."

I continued to work with Jennifer on how to accomplish her next steps. She took a part-time job in the veterinary hospital acquiring skills and knowledge while still maintaining her accounting position. Two years later, she had saved up enough money to resign from her accounting job. And her love of animals coupled with all her accounting and business skills allowed her to open a pet care service. She is now happier than ever. She is living her dream.

||||||||||||||||||||||||||||||||||||||||||||||||||||||||||

EXERCISES

Faith is taking the first step even when you don't see the whole staircase.
—Martin Luther King, Jr.

What prayers have you been making lately?

_____

_____

_____

_____

What feelings, emotions, ideas, and inspirations have you been connected with? What have you been receiving?

_____

_____

_____

Have you connected with any Divine helpers? If yes, name and describe each one.

_____

_____

_____

How do you connect with God? Explain.

_____

_____

_____

Chapter 19

Assemble Your Divine Support Team on Earth

"Make your own Bible. Select and collect all the words and sentences that in your reading have been like the blast of triumph out of Shakespeare, Seneca, Moses, John and Paul."
— Ralph Waldo Emerson

Start a group, even a group of one…you! Get to know yourself better. Get in touch with your spirit—that magnificent you that has been hiding in order to appease others. As you become acquainted with your spirit again, you will notice a refreshing knowing about your truth. Your life will make sense. You will be able to source the power within you that was hidden and is dying to come out. This power is the power of God. Remember we are all connected. We are all one! And as you draw upon this power you can be the catalyst for peace and love. You can be a leader in your own and perfect way. It doesn't matter how much or little you may think you're helping, it's always huge!

And as you realize the power within and feel guided, then reach out to others, but only to those who want to be enlightened. Only to those who want to create the peace and love themselves. Remember we don't want to convince anyone. We want to be available to those who need a helping hand from one side of the bridge to the other. Feel free to use this book with others by creating groups meeting weekly, monthly or as often as you like. The point is that we want to create a spiritual revolution. A spiritual revolution of peace and love. One that eventually everyone wants to partake in. Let's roll with it. Let's do it together. Let's do it for our spirit!

Believe me, you are not alone. There are others in your situation, waiting to be with you! So start looking with your spiritual eyes!

Tina's Spiritual Circle

As I began to evolve, I became guilt free and self-assured with my spirituality. I got to the point that nothing anyone said or tried in order to convince me otherwise, impacted me in any way. Today, I could care less what people think or say about me. However, lots of my clients and students have not reached this level of confidence yet. I realized that they are at the crucial point of breaking free. And so my guides and angels led me to create retreats and classes for like-minded people who could come together to support each other and evolve spiritually.

One of these groups is what I call, "Tina's Spiritual Circle." In this group many people can be themselves and honor one another no matter where they are in their spiritual evolution. We pray, meditate, laugh, cry, chant, sing, retreat, and have fun with each other. This group has evolved in such a profound way that I've witnessed miracles among the participants. They have been there for each other in all times, but especially in times of need. Great friendships have formed. And as these friendships grow, I see spiritual growth among the members of the group. The depth of their relationships are so intense and yet gentle. It's like witnessing the coming together of spiritual sisters and brothers. How rewarding it is to be observer and participant as well. I learn from them all the time as they from me. It's a win-win situation. And I am so honored for the Great Spirit to have brought us together.

How to Connect with Your Divine Support Team on Earth

You may experience rejection when you come out. That's what makes it so important to have a support person or a group already in place. This will help you know that you are not alone. In fact, this book is reaching a multitude of people in similar situations. It should comfort you to know that others in the world are walking beside you.

When I first emerged from my spiritual closet, I sought out groups, seminars, classes, people that believed the way I did. This made it so much easier for me to continue on the spiritual path. There was no one to judge me. No one to ridicule me. No one to burst my bubble. Later, as I started my practice, I created special classes for people to explore their spirituality. This made it easier for others to feel safe and secure in their belief system. People still come and feel connected.

Surround yourself with the right people—people who will enhance and support your journey. Check out your local listings, the internet, and newspapers for like-minded groups or spirituality classes. If you live in a small town, seek people online. Identify spiritual people you admire. This is an important step in your spiritual evolution. Like-minded people create love, respect and support of your journey.

Places to look for like-minded people:

- Schools
- Associations
- Friends
- Colleagues
- Acquaintances
- Newspapers
- Internet

Remember that brainstorming allows you to open the imagination channels in your mind for possibilities. Although you may think one way now, other options may occur to you later. Let yourself evolve. Be open to opportunities.

On the other hand, continuing your relationships with your existing circle of people may not be in your best interest. So, just as you're gravitating toward like-minded people, you will also be transitioning away from people, places, and things that do not serve you. The fact of the matter is you're not serving them either, so be the one who knows better and take action. This means, if you disagree with someone and they have thousands of opinions then there's no need to convince them. Move on! If others disagree with you, you don't want their thoughts and energies interrupting your process. Figure out your spiritual path from within and join with like-minded people.

Initially you may need assistance to clear old religious emotional patterns and beliefs that no longer serve you. Trust that the spiritual process will happen for your highest good and the highest good of all. You are always connected to your higher power and so go with the flow. Miracles will happen.

Happiness starts from the inside and it spreads to the outside. If you are happy and complete at the core, then it's very difficult for any negativity to permeate. Be proud of the person you are.

But in the process, it's also compassionate to realize that everyone is trying the best they can. Remember that those who condemn you are still asleep. Others are almost awake. They just keep hitting the spiritual snooze button. They will be waking up at their own pace and a day will come when they too shall awaken and see the Light. It has taken this long for you, so honor and hold space for others to go through their spiritual evolution at their own rhythm and speed. Speak your truth mindfully and honorably without judging or offending others so you can progress to your new spiritual you. Others may need more time. What would God or Jesus do? Love them.

Finding Your Place

An old friend of mine contacted me and said that she recently moved to a distant state because of her husband's job relocation. She felt so out of place in this environment. She mentioned that everyone was so closed-minded spiritually and she was concerned for her daughters to live there.

"They are going to burn me at the stake Tina," Sarah said. "I've been here six months and I haven't unpacked yet because I want to leave!"

"Is it really that bad?" I asked.

"Yes! They all think alike and are not open whatsoever!"

"Well, I believe there is a reason why you're there. You are not the only one feeling this way. Your job is to locate like-minded people and do your healing work. Find the gifts around you."

"A group? I don't know anyone here. Gifts? What gifts? There is nothing here!" Sarah complained.

"You just moved to this part of the country. Give it some time. But keep your ears and eyes open. There are others like you. There is definitely a spiritual reason for your being there. Find out and move on it," I advised.

After several months, Sarah contacted me with great news. "Hey Tina," she said, "I started going to a group and I can't believe how easy it was."

"Really? Tell me more."

"Well when you told me to keep my ears and eyes open, I decided to do just that. Everywhere I went from then on, I would just scan all the people who were in my day. I was consciously doing this all the time until I met Rebecca. She is just like us Tina! A group has been meeting at her place, and now we are growing each week. There is so much opportunity for me to do my healing work here. So many people are thirsty for this type of experience. I'm having so much fun! You were right Tina. I had to open up and see the gifts around me."

"So did you unpack yet?" I asked

Jennifer busted out laughing hysterically!

Support, create and/or join groups that promote peace and love. Peace and love are truly contagious. Let's create more.

‖‖‖

EXERCISES

"If we could look into the secret history of our enemies, we should find in each person's life, sorrow and suffering enough to disarm all hostilities."
—Henry Wadsworth Longfellow

What groups that you can pursue exist in your area?

_____

_____

_____

_____

Research and list groups available:

Town:_____

_____

State: _____

_____

Internet:_____

_____

Other: _____

_____

If there are none, create your own group. Imagine or visualize it.
Name the people you would like to participate in this group:

_____

_____

_____

What is the maximum number of members? When the maximum is reached, will that spin off to another group?

_____

How many times a month would you meet?

_____

What agenda items would you include? (Examples: opening sacred space, meditation, ceremony, spiritual activity, closing sacred space)

_____

_____

_____

Where will this group be held?

_____

If there are costs involved, how will they be handled?

_____

_____

_____

Bonus: Download free exercises, meditations, tips, etc. at
*www.**TinaSacchi**.com*

Notes

Notes

Chapter 20

Be the Spiritual Peace You Seek One Spiritual Step at a Time

"Man does not weave this web of life. He is merely a strand of it. Whatever he does to the web, he does to himself. All things are bound together. All things connect."
—Chief Seattle

We Are All Connected. We Are One.

Remember that God is omnipresent—present in all places at all times—existing in stones, plants, animals, and within us. See God within you. Feel God within you. Know that God is within you. You were never separated. Always together. Always one. We are all one.

This is not a new concept. In fact, indigenous cultures around the world believe this. From Native Americans to other peoples, they have always had the faith and belief that we are one. As a matter of fact it's a narrow, egotistical, and ignorant point of view to believe that there is separation or that a certain religion is the only way.

Indigenous people live in every region of the world and in different climates ranging from Arctic cold to Amazonian heat. What keeps them going is faith in a Higher Power and that the sacredness of the earth is a valuable source not only for food and health but for spirituality. They connect with the earth and thus connect to God in an innate way, an instinctive way—a way that the modern civilization has lost or forgotten. Although each indigenous culture is distinct and unique, they all have a common respect and honor for the earth which is an interchangeable belief in God.

I had the honor and pleasure to experience various people from different tribes around the world. A couple of years ago I met three loving medicine men from Sierra Nevada de Santa Marta from Colombia, South America. They conducted a beautiful ceremony healing the Earth and its inhabitants. Balancing the spiritual and ecological world is their sacred task.

Being in their presence brought so much joy to my heart, connecting it with my spiritual purpose even deeper. They spoke neither English nor formal Spanish. However our souls spoke to each other without words.

They are not bombarded with technology since that is not how they live. They live simply, high in the mountains in primitive form, connecting within to the earth with God. Their message was clear: go within and see and feel God. And once you feel God, you know what matters. Everything else that is unimportant will seem trivial.

We are all one.

Imagine various ice sculptures carved to look like swans and trees and butterflies and children. They all seem so distinct, so different. Now turn up the heat. Turn on love. They all start melting and melding together. What you get is something you cannot differentiate… we are all the same….we are all one!

What God has tried to convey to us through various masters is much deeper than what a church, mosque, or synagogue is conveying. The message has gotten lost somewhere. But if we go deeper into the religion, we will all get to the same place… the hub of the Ferris wheel. Many paths, many spokes lead to our Creator. No one way is the right way. We can be free-thinking religious people who believe there are many paths that lead to God.

Let Peace Begin with Us

Spirituality and spiritual peace begin within us first so that we can spread and touch others. It's about giving the way we want to receive. Whatever we give out will come back to us—what goes around comes around. This is Universal law. Think about how you can be the source for another of whatever you want to bring to your own life. That which you give away will come back to you. Making someone happy with honest and sincere intention, is the fastest way to happiness since what you choose to give to another, you give to yourself. **This is the opposite of being hypocritical: you put on a false appearance of virtue and contradict your stated beliefs or feelings through your actions. Rather, it's about having love in your heart from neither obligation nor fear.**

Life is happening through you and not to you. The world is being done by you and not to you. You are the one that needs to find peace within. Although it is true that you give to others the way you want to receive, it is also true that you must give to yourself. If patience is what you need, then patience is what you do for yourself. If forgiveness is what you need then forgiveness is what you do for yourself. Find what you need and do it for yourself. You are in control of feeling and being just the way you want. Your spirit has an unlimited field of possibilities. Find the peace and have the peace, faith and belief in yourself to guide you through your spiritual development.

Not a Christian but Christ-like

Sometimes other cultures, traditions, and religions can help us go deeper into our own spirituality. We mustn't dismiss others' points of view without understanding their core. There had to be a reason for the initial start of the belief or religion. As we peel away the layers, we can discover the treasure in that belief system and perhaps we can understand and use the teachings for our own growth.

For years, being surrounded by many Christians including me, one of my Jewish friends asked her parents for a Christmas tree. And for years they declined. When she got her own apartment, she decided to get a tree, and her parents were astounded. She told them that she wanted to be part of the culture, the beauty it provided with all the lights on, and the happiness it brought to her. More importantly, to her it wasn't a symbol of Jesus. Rather, it was a symbol of Christ or the Messiah whose appearance is prophesied in the Old Testament.

They were caught off guard. This event was the start of wonderful discussions about Judaism for the whole family. They engaged in deep conversations each time they met. As a matter of fact, they realized that there was a lot about their religion they didn't know and so this created a mission to obtain some answers. In the process, they learned about Christianity, the origin of Christmas and more. They also bonded more strongly as a family as a result.

Sometimes God nudges us in a roundabout way to get in touch with ourselves and our loved ones on a deeper level to demonstrate how we truly all are connected.

Embracing More Than One Way

At the age of 21, my client, Romona, was attending my spirituality classes, trying to gain some clarity. She was raised Catholic and Native American due to the influence of her dad and mom, respectively—an interesting combination to say the least. The main belief for both views is that there is a higher power. The conflicts arose in the areas of attending church—the connection to God from the Catholic perspective—versus honoring the earth through ceremony—the Native American way.

Ramona lived with this difference between her mom and dad. She loved both parents, but she was always asked to take sides. She realized the benefits inherent in both religions along with some disadvantages. In turmoil, she came in for a private appointment.

"I love both my parents, but I can't take this anymore. They each want me to agree with them and I can't," she said.

"What can't you do Ramona?"

"I can't take sides. I've been secretly agreeing with each one to keep the peace, but now they are confronting me at the same time."

"What will it take for you to tell them exactly what you believe from each spiritual perspective and that you will honor both religions in your own way?"

"What do you mean?" She looked puzzled.

"There is room for both Ramona. You don't have to totally disagree with either religion. You can extract the teachings and the beliefs that you resonate with and leave the rest. You can create your own flavor, your own connection."

"I can do that?"

"Of course you can! That's what makes it so powerful to live a spiritual life. We each connect in our own way."

I worked with Ramona by having her create a list of all the things she loved about each belief system. Her two lists were extensive. Then I had her combine all these positive aspects on one page.

"So how would it feel to live a spiritual life with all these qualities?" I asked.

"That would be awesome."

"When can you give yourself permission to do so?"

"Now. But what about my parents?"

"Tell them how much you love them and show them the qualities you honor about each viewpoint. Keep reassuring them that you appreciate each one for giving you the various perspectives. And then ask for their love and support so you can integrate what you believe in. Also let them know that they do have loving hearts. Since they were open enough to marry each other from different worlds, ask them to be open to your spiritual growth."

It took Ramona a little time to express to each parent her decision and stance, but not as long as she had thought. After all, if her parents were open enough to marry each other in spite of different faiths, there was a place to create the space for their daughter. They allowed themselves to embrace each other's beliefs with love and peace.

Creating Your Own Path. . . .

By now I hope you have a better sense of your spiritual path. If you don't have a complete picture, no worries! Spirituality is an evolution not a destination. Take it one step at a time. For some there will be an automatic knowing of what needs to be done although guidance and steps are needed. For others, it is a huge step that means enormous change. In any case, know that you are not alone and you don't have to abandon your religion or beliefs altogether.

If your heart is telling you that a change is necessary, then take your heart's lead. If you feel obligated or hypocritical, then take a moment and a breath to figure out what's next. Take baby steps. One step, that will lead you to another step and then to another.

Sometimes change is difficult even though we know in our core that it is necessary. We humans get stuck in routines. They seem easier to live through than change at times. However know that if you're reading this book, somewhere inside you there is a yearning for authentic spirituality in your life. Somewhere within yourself, you ache to be a better person, a bona fide spiritual being. The good news is that you can walk both worlds until you figure it out. And what is the worst case scenario? You can always go back to your old religion. You can!

As I outgrew some parts of my Catholic upbringing, I also extracted and carried over certain beliefs and traditions that were important for my spirituality. One that I still hold in my heart today is the belief in Saints; they are part of my Divine support team. I call upon various Saints such as Saint Anthony, Saint Joseph, and Saint Francis, to name a few. I also believe in coming together as a community or a spiritual circle in ceremony and in service. In the Catholic religion that is done every week at mass. Today, I gather in ceremony when my spirit calls for it. There is no right or wrong way from my point of view. I also believe in certain traditions such as Christmas and Easter. As I explained earlier, I used to follow the whole 40 day ritual of Lent. Now I mindfully go through that period with intentional giving to others rather than fasting, abstinence, and penitence. If I feel like fasting or cleansing, I don't need to wait for Lent. I follow my spiritual cues.

I have established a tradition in my house on specific holidays to sit down with my kids and husband and discuss what the holiday means to each one of us, how the holiday originated, the different beliefs surrounding the holiday around the world, and so on. We truly get more out of this than all the sermons I listened to in church.

IIIIIIIIIIIIIIIIIIIIIIIIIIIIIIIIIIIIIIIIIIIIIIIIIIIII

EXERCISES

If you judge people, you have no time to love them.
—Mother Teresa

How can you be the spiritual peace that you seek in your world?

_____

_____

_____

Do you believe that we are all connected? Explain.

_____

_____

_____

What parts of your old religion do you want to hold onto and incorporate into your spirituality and why?

_____

_____

_____

_____

Bonus: Download free exercises, meditations, tips, etc. at
*www.**TinaSacchi**.com*

||||||||||||||||||||||||||||||||||||||||||||||||||

Notes

Notes

Chapter 21

Who Is Walking with Me?

"In a gentle way, you can shake the world."
—Mahatma Gandhi

onnecting with spirituality instead of religion may seem like a regrettable move at first due to others' judgments; but, if dealt with correctly, the emotional rollercoaster eventually becomes a cleansing process.

There is a spiritual and fulfilling future waiting for you. Once you find a safe environment and positive support system, you will evolve intuitively. Your spirit will guide you. You have a choice as to the kind of person you want to be and who you want to become. Finding peace and joy in your beliefs is your birthright. Others may judge and condemn you, but that's their issue. Living a spiritual life is normal and you are not alone. Create a new life now, one that you define for yourself!

What Matters

Over the years in my hypnotherapy work, I have helped hundreds of clients and students regress to past and in-between lives—the time and space between incarnations. Some people may call it heaven. (If past life regression is something you don't believe in, then practice non-judgment right here and now and hold space for my belief. After all that is what spiritual people do. They honor others in their beliefs. So you are being spiritually tested right now!) Through hypnotherapy, we have accessed purposes for their past lives and learned that many times their main purpose was not accomplished during a specific lifetime. They had to come back again and for some, many times, to complete their purpose.

At your death, no one will ask you why you didn't go to church on a particular Sunday in September 1978. Nor will there be a question as to why you only said one Hail Mary prayer on that confession on a Friday in 1998. But there are some questions you will ask of yourself since you are connected to God and we are all one are:

- Did I do what I came here to do?
- Did I allow myself to be happy?

Two important issues are captured in these simple questions: your spiritual purpose and love.

First of all, your spiritual purpose is divinely perfect and can only produce good things such as love, harmony, joy, serenity, and peace.

Secondly, if you didn't allow yourself happiness, this means you also did not give anyone else happiness. Instead, you gave them grief and misery. Making someone happy is the fastest way to happiness. But this does not mean that you will sacrifice your spiritual truth and whimsically and go out of your way so you can put a smile on someone's face. Rather, it means that with truth and integrity and being guided with your heart and spirit that you spread love and joy and it will come back to you.

There is a spiritual solution to everyone issue, situation, and problem. The solution is within you. Seek God within you.

Hold Your Head Up

Stand tall and proud. If you are confronted by critical people, just walk away. It doesn't make sense to convince anyone who is not ready to hear what you have to say or what you believe in. Just remember that it took you all this time to get to this point of change. Others need to catch up, that's all. Have faith that everyone will be enlightened in Divine timing, and that this is your Divine time to Light up!

When you do come out and hold your head up high in your spiritual faith you will feel liberation from all the hidden constraints that kept you in your closet. Don't ever give up. It gets easier as your new circle of friends support you on your spiritual path. Don't ever lose sight of yourself. It may take some time for your family to accept your beliefs. However rest assured that at the end of the day, moreover at the end of your lifetime, you will recognize that living your spiritual life is not about what everyone else thinks and feels. It is about you being honest and true with your spirit!

My Journey

As you know, I was raised in a strict Italian Catholic family. My parents were determined that I follow in their footsteps— no deviation whatsoever especially when it came to religion! I attended Catholic schools my whole life. Throughout those years, I really felt a real closeness to God. As a matter of fact, in the sixth grade I believed I would become a nun someday so that I could touch others spiritually. I looked up to my sixth grade teacher, Sister Mary. She was funny, religious and beautiful inside and out. I remember feeling that I wanted to be closer to God on a deeper level, and becoming a nun like her would do that for me. On the other hand, I looked at all the rules and regulations that the church placed on everyone, and I became disillusioned with the whole concept of serving God in this very structured way.

Time passed and I began to feel that a lot of the church's rules—purgatory and limbo, confession, an unmarried, priesthood that remained celibate, annulment, self-abnegation during Lent—and its stance on birth control and divorce were outdated. The church just didn't do it for me any longer. Even in the search to find the "right" church, I saw so much hypocrisy around me. Some people just didn't practice what they preached. They attended services diligently and paid lip service to a higher good, but then would act out in the outside world, hurting and judging others. Again all these religions were not up to date and they had little to do with my true understanding of religion which is based on loving others.

I became a spiritual person who lived in the closet, attending church services only when I needed to for rituals such as weddings, funerals, and baptisms. Sundays became our sacred family time together. That to me was spiritual—to create wonderful, loving memories with each other.

As I slowly phased out of Catholicism, I became more certain of my true identity. I started to discover who I really was. My spiritual teaching of students and clients reaffirmed who I was and my life's purpose. The more I surrounded myself with like- minded friends, the more I became confident, self-assured, and enthusiastic about my spirituality.

As I slowly transitioned from religion to my spiritual path, some family members began drifting away. The closeness we once had was lost. It was a different type of closeness—loving, because they are wonderful human beings, but spiritually restricting. I was unable to grow spiritually in those relationships. Some family members like my brother and his wife didn't fully get what I was all about. But they were very supportive, nonetheless, because they believed in me. They believed in my spirit. And even though we were not on the same page spiritually, I didn't feel confined or restricted by them.

At first it was weird not having people I was used to spend time with around me. But over time, I realized that their absence created space for me. It gave me more time to pursue my spiritual path and to be with like-minded people. The arguments and phone calls that consumed so much time and energy before were now virtually non-existent. There was no longer a need for me to escape any religious conversations or the intrusive questions my disgruntled relatives posed.

Today, I am free! Free from having to explain or justify my spiritual stance. When these relatives call and ask to speak to my children or husband, I respect them and honor their path. Internally I am grateful for how my past experiences with them taught me lessons and gave me opportunities. And even if they think I am irrational in my spiritual ways—and I know some of them do think this—so be it. Their opinion of me is none of my business!

And so I slowly created my family. My spiritual family. My husband began waking up as time went on. His support is tremendous. He gets the big picture although the details may be nebulous for him. It doesn't matter. He is my biggest fan. We are raising our children into spirituality. And I wish that they will continue to flourish the way they are right now—confident, self-assured and enthusiastic about God. My spiritual family also includes my students, clients, and mentees. My spiritual family reinforces me in staying out of the closet and continuing on my spiritual path.

Helping Others on Their Way

They say that God sends you the people He knows you can help. And boy have I been helping many people like me who have been living in their spiritual closet and looking for a nudge, guidance, and assistance in getting out!

At age 21, Sue came to me without the intention of coming out spiritually. The only thing she knew was that she was not sleeping at night and was experiencing pain all over her body. That was it.

"So why are you here Sue?" I asked

"I can't sleep at night due to my physical pain. I feel all my muscles hurting all the time. My doctors can't find anything wrong with me, which makes me so mad since I am hurting. So I decided to seek alternative help. That's why I am here to see you."

"How long have you been this way?"

"It started about 5 years ago with occasional pain, and it has increased ever since. I haven't slept right in a year. I feel like a zombie. It gets really hard for me to go to school and study or finish my homework assignments. Sometimes I can't even drive. I often have to ask a friend to drive me to school. And it's difficult for me to keep a job because I never know how I am going to feel on a specific day."

"What happened five years ago?"

"I can't think of anything major. No car accidents or anything like that."

"What about life event changes? Things that changed in your daily routine?" I asked.

Concentrating intently, Sue recounted, "The only thing I can think of is that my Dad became the leading minister of our church about six years ago. He went from being a church member to having to run the whole church."

"Did the fact that your dad was in a different position change anything for you?"

"Yes it did. He didn't have any time for my brothers and me any longer. We were expected to attend all these religious services and events. They took up all our time! I had to give up my social activities to conform to his minister obligations. It was crazy! My mom didn't care. She was totally happy to be Mrs. Minister! She would always say that I was selfish to be thinking of myself and not for my father. That he was doing it all for us!

"And you know Tina, I really don't believe in religion anymore. I mean there is a God, but I don't feel that God the way my church does any longer. I haven't told anyone, or else I would be put to shame. I feel that I would be a failure to my dad, especially since he has such a huge position and thousands of church members look up to him."

I found the hot button. And so with hypnosis, I regressed Sue to the root cause so we could gain some clarity on her issues. She realized that by having physical pain, many times she was excused from continuing her duties with her Mom and Dad. She was able to escape from it all. This included escaping from attending a church and practicing a religion she no longer believed in. It became the "Sue story" or "Sue excuse." Her parents and friends knew about her pain and felt compassion toward her so they left her alone and would not question why she was not attending any church services or events.

Unconsciously this worked great with the church and religious obligations, but it carried over to other parts of Sue's life. She wasn't living her truth. She was escaping everything by hiding behind her pain. Everything else in her life including her future suffered along too. She was hiding in the spiritual closet with her beliefs.

We proceeded to work through many of the layers of pain she had accumulated. Through various alternative healing techniques, we finally shifted the pain energy out of her field and replaced it with self-esteem and the confidence that she has the right to live her life for herself and not for others.

Sue's parents were devastated when she first approached them with her truth. But they were truly loving people—a beautiful quality with which they infused their church—and they witnessed Sue's dramatic improvement. So over time, they became somewhat supportive. I have continued to mentor Sue, and she now has a metaphysical practice which is thriving. Her pain is her history.

‖‖‖

EXERCISES

"I only went out for a walk, and finally concluded to stay out
till sundown, for going out, I found, was really going in."
—John Muir

Imagine that today is your last day on earth. How would you answer each of the following questions?

Did I do what I came here to do? Explain.

_____

_____

_____

Did I allow myself to be happy? Explain

_____

_____

_____

_____

Did I live openly and spiritually?

_____

_____

_____

_____

If today was not your last day and you were given more time on Earth, what changes would you make and why?

_____

_____

_____

Bonus: Download free exercises, meditations, tips, etc. at
*www.**TinaSacchi**.com*

Notes

Notes

Chapter 22

Dream Spiritual Peace and Love into Being

"There is nothing like a dream to create the future."
—Victor Hugo

There has never been a better time than now to make the changes you want to make in order for you to live a spiritual life. The freedom we have now compared to yesteryears and yester-centuries is enormous. Radiate your light, which will ignite others' light. Remember we are all one.

Be the example for our people, for our children of now and of the future. Let them know that it's perfectly fine to live spiritually and free rather than confined religiously with guilt. Let's all rise and celebrate life without conditions, restrictions, hindrances. Let's all dream peace and love into being. Are you with me?

There has never been a better time to be on this earth.... to rise...start a new life....radiate the life... truth...of possibilities....crawl out of the past...turn it all around....

celebrate life…we've been in preparation for this time…step into the whole of we are.

Coexistence

We all need to be open to others' ways of connecting spiritually whether it's in a religious way or other. This is so important in order for our human race, to evolve. We must learn to be open to other people's traditions, cultures, race, creed, sexual orientation, religion, so long as it doesn't promote hurting or killing others or damaging our planet. And if the latter is happening, we enlighten with peace and love not war. With kindness. The bottom line is that we must love ourselves unconditionally and in turn we then can love others the same way too.

Remember the only limits there are, are those you create. I'm calling out you to think differently. Think with your heart and not your head.

This is a call to all. To all women and men. A call to the human race. A call from the Great Spirit for us to unite so that we can move forward in peace and with love. What would God do in your place?

Our time has come, my fellow Earth dwellers. It's our time to make a difference and shine our light, the light of our spirit, the light of God. There can be no more excuses, no more powerless or cookie-cutter leaders. We must stand together to tell the world what is right and what is wrong. We can no longer settle for status quo, or continue the way we've always done things. Let us all come together and ignite our souls and passion to create the beautiful, loving world we know is possible. It must start with us, individually. And those of us who are answering the call can assist others to do so, too.

I envision this and more. I also see groups forming around the world to tell all those individuals who have continually tried to engage us in their fear to "back off!" Religion hasn't been working for thousands of years, and it's not working now. So back off! Hate and war don't create peace. They never have and they never will. History confirms this. For thousands of years, we've been fighting and killing in the name of religious beliefs and in the name of God. But just look at the irony of it. We believe in God, the almighty, so we're killing other beings in His name. We're fomenting intolerance and clinging to the concept that my way is the only right way. How ridiculous!

Only love can attract more love and peace. Fear might have worked once upon a time, but it does not work any longer. All you leaders who wield the weapon of fear are acting out of fear, yourselves. You are insecure! I challenge each of you to transform this illusion of fear. F.E.A.R. is nothing more than False Evidence Appearing Real. Stop creating false evidence and telling others it's real. We are not ignorant; we know it is not real. So stop all the nonsense. You've insulted us with your attitude and actions. We are smarter, and much more loving than that.

I challenge all leaders to end the ways of the past; begin embracing positive ideals, such as love, peace, understanding, and harmony to create our future. I challenge leaders to create other loving leaders, rather than docile sheep followers. We don't need more followers. We need more spiritual leaders now to help sculpt our world into the loving shape it can and must embody. We need more leaders and masters to help those in need of some help to climb out of the black hole that humanity has created.

Blessings to YOU!

To find out more about Tina Sacchi, her availability as a speaker, retreat facilitator, products, services, healthy tips, recipes, free podcasts from her international radio shows, please visit her website.

Bonus: Download free exercises, meditations, tips, etc. at

www.TinaSacchi.com

Some of Tina's best-selling audios include:

I Sleep, Sleep, Sleep Soundly Now
(Complete audio set: Preparing to Sleep Checklist,
Meditation, and Hypnotherapy/Hypnosis)

I Decide and I Create the Body I Want
Weight Management Hypnotherapy with
A Mind-Body-Spirit-Emotional Connection

Serenity: A Suite of Four Guided Imagery Meditations

Connecting With Ascended Masters,
Guides, Angels and Light Beings Meditation

Survive Cancer Now
The Hypnotherapy way to Replace Dis-ease
with Excellent Health, Happiness, and Love

Supere El Cáncer Ahora
Reemplace el cáncer con un excelente estado
de salud, felicidad, y amor usando hipnoterapia

Tina Sacchi is a holistic & spiritual author, speaker, and teacher. Through her work, she has coached and helped people emerge and make a smooth transition to their passion. She is also the creator of a series of highly successful meditation and hypnotherapy CDs that have consistently remained on Amazon bestseller lists in their categories. She is an ongoing writer for various publications and is a radio personality, hosting her own programs. Learn more about Tina through her website: www.TinaSacchi.com

Tina is available in-person, via phone, and voice over IP
(VoIP) services such as Skype, FaceTime, etc.

Bulk ordering rates are available with all products.

We want love and peace now! All we are saying is, "Give peace a chance." Religion is not doing this. Spirituality will accomplish it.

So who is with me?

I'm moving forward, with or without you — but I would much prefer it if you'd join me on this enormous, essential mission. I'm acting for love. I'm living for peace. Who's walking with me?

Peace and love,
Tina